Small Portion

Small Portion

A "dwarf" finds God in the

struggle for normality

Sue Phillips

Highland Books

First published in 1997 by Highland Books, 2 High Pines, Knoll Road, Godalming, Surrey, GU7 2EP.

Cover Design by Sally Maltby

British Library Cataloguing-in-Publication Data.   A catalogue record for this book is available from the British Library.   ISBN: 1 897913 34 6

Printed in Great Britain by Caledonian International Book Manufacturing Limited, Glasgow.

Dedication

This book is dedicated to the memory
of two dear friends:

Rosalie Curran
who taught me to laugh at being small

Win Davies
a dear friend and inspiration for 40 years

Yet this I call to mind and therefore I have hope.

Because of the Lord's great love we are not consumed, for his compassions never fail. They are new every morning; great is your faithfulness.

I say to myself, 'the Lord is my portion; therefore I will wait for Him.'

The Lord is good to those who hope is in him, to the one who seeks him;

It is good to wait quietly for the salvation of the Lord.

It is good for a man to bear the yoke while he is young.

Lamentations 3: 21-27

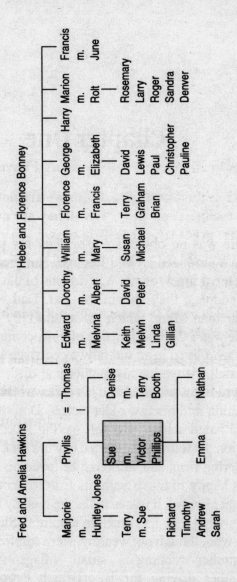

Chapter One

There was no obvious reason why my parents should have produced a child like me. No family history, no sign of anything wrong, it was just one of those things. Like many couples, they met in the war. Dad was five years younger than Mum, which made him only 18 when they met. He was a Cornish lad, one of nine, coming from a poor family who lived in an old railway carriage at Sticker, near St. Austell. At twelve his mother had died, worn out with having so many children and his care was taken over by his Aunt Edith and his two older sisters, Dorothy and Florrie. He had hated school, and left having received very little education. At fourteen he started to work for Costains, a civil engineering firm, and, although he loved his family dearly, he was happy to move with his firm to Scotland and then Yate, near Bristol. It was here that he met my mum. It would not seem that they had much in common. She came from a family who, though not wealthy, were comfortably off – my grandmother running a small village shop and my grandfather driving for BP (British Petroleum). Mum, herself, was a primary school teacher. At that time when she left school in 1938, you could train to teach by working with another teacher for a year and then you were classed as an uncertified teacher – this was the way my mother started to teach. Soon after they met, Dad was called up into the Army – the Royal Engineers. He saw active service in France and Germany. Two of his elder brothers, Edward and Bill, were prisoners of war, and his younger brother, Harry, was killed soon after he joined up.

I know my father loved the family atmosphere he found at "Crofton" with my amiable grandfather, my grandmother and my Auntie Marjorie, who was engaged to be married to Huntley at that time. When my parents married in 1946 Dad was in the Army and they remained living at Crofton for several years until Dad was demobbed. It was no hardship for my father to live with his in-laws – he loved them dearly.

In 1948, I was born. Towards the end of my mother's pregnancy she was quite ill, and was so relieved when the birth was over that she did not really grieve for my stillborn twin brother. She was so weak and ill that she did not take me out for nearly six months and it was fortunate that my grandmother was on hand to help. Auntie Marjorie by this time had a three year old son, Terry, but she lived just down the road, so the family remained close. My mother had worries about me from the start. She thought I did not turn my head to one side as easily as I did the other, my thumb nails were fat and wide, and I would not feed. When I started to walk at about 12 months I waddled from side to side. Mum took me to the doctor who thought that it could be due to the bulky terry nappy, as I was quite small; he told Mum to take me back when I was out of nappies.

Auntie Marjorie had had problems with Terry and his walking and had been referred to a consultant who had advised raises in his shoes which had cured the problem. Mum tried to put my problems out of her mind hoping that they could be cured as easily as had Terry's.

At eighteen months, I was out of nappies, but still waddling. Mum took me back to the doctor, who decided to refer me to the same consultant that Terry had seen, Mr. Eyre Brook. Dr. Hartill wrote a very long letter to Mr. Eyre Brook, I sat patiently on my mother's lap, watching him write. He wrote very slowly and then re-read the letter dotting every 'i' and crossing every 't'. At last I gave a big sigh and said "Well, if we wait here much longer it will be dinner time." which embarassed my mother, but made the doctor laugh.

We were able to see Mr. Eyre Brook at a local clinic and off we went on the appointed day. My mother had no idea what he was going to say and she told me a long time later that after her visit she went to bed crying and woke every morning convinced that she had had a nightmare, only to realise as she woke fully that this was no nightmare. She had a daughter who had pseudoachondroplasia, or as the world would say, dwarfism. The only dwarfs she had seen were in a circus, figures of fun. What would happen to her daughter? How cruel would the world be to her? Mr. Eyre Brook had pulled no punches. He told her straightaway that I would never grow to be a great deal bigger, that I could well have problems with my spine and legs bending, and these could be helped surgically, but that no operation or medicine would make me grow.

Mum took me home, feeling that her world had crashed. She was a strong Christian, as were my grandparents, and a vast amount of prayers went up asking for a miracle. After a while, Mum, Dad, Nanny and Grampy began to get used to the idea. They all loved me and were determined to do the best for me. There was not going to be a circus life for me. Mum did not know how to bring up a disabled child, her experience was with 'normal' children, so that is how I was treated.

When I was two we moved to a council house – a prefab, and there my sister, Denise, was born when I was five. She was everything I wasn't, blonde, blue-eyed, tall, and I loved her to bits. Dr. Hartill convinced me that my mother just could not manage at home without me and made a big play of asking the school if I could start two weeks later than the others, so that I could help my mother with the new baby. Perhaps this was the reason that I can never remember being jealous of her. The local school head teacher, Miss Bannister had taught with my mother, so when I was five Mum took me along to school and Miss Bannister pretended not to notice that I had something wrong with me and should really have gone to a 'special school'. By the time it was picked up, I had proved that I was coping perfectly well and was allowed to stay there.

I continued to see Mr. Eyre Book at regular intervals and I hated that. Mum used to take me on the bus – this entailed pushing me in my pushchair to the bus stop in the town, then folding up the chair, which took quite a while, lifting it and me on the bus, going into Bristol, and then pushing me up St.Michael's Hill to the Children's Hospital. At the start of the day, when I realised I had to go to see Mr. Eyre Brook I would hide under the dining room table, crying loudly. I can remember being convinced that Mum would not know where I was and would go without me. (Apart from the fact that she could see me under the table cloth, I am sure that not only Mum but the neighbours could hear me crying and there would have been little point in her going to the hospital without me!)

I kept on crying until we had actually finished our appointment – when Mum would take me into the Broadmead shopping area in Bristol and buy me a toy for being a good girl!

In addition to being small, my legs began to bow, as did my spine. I went into hospital when I was six to have my legs straightened. I stayed in for one month as they did some tests to see if they could determine why I was like I was, but nothing concrete was ever found. My legs were straighter, but no stronger. I have never been able to walk any distance as I have very loose joints which begin to rub and ache after too much exercise and I was forced to go everywhere by pushchair.

As I got older and did not want Mum taking me to school I rode my three-wheeled bike – flying down a steep hill to get to school and persuading the boys to push me up it on the way home! My mother had quite a nervous disposition and I am sure, now I am a mother myself, that her instincts were to cushion me against life. Thankfully she did not do this but pushed me out into the world with all the other children.

When I was about 9 we went to Cornwall. Dad's sister Dorothy, a widow, was dying of cancer and we went to see her in hospital in Plymouth on the way down. We then went on to my Aunt Florrie's. She lived in a cottage on a small holding, with her three sons. Terry, Graham and Brian and Dorothy's son, Peter. Her husband, Uncle Demps, worked long hours as a crane driver as well as looking after the animals. Mum and Dad had never told anyone in Cornwall that there was anything wrong with me. They wanted me accepted as I was. My cousins were going over the fields to play, so I wanted to go too. My mum said I could and Denise tagged along with me. Auntie Florrie was horrified and worried that I would fall. Mum just said if I did I would pick myself up again and that set the scene for my acceptance as an individual by my Cornish relaties; I did not ask for special treatment and I did not get it. In my teens I used to go and stay with Auntie Florrie and Uncle Demps for a few weeks each summer and they used to say while I was there I was the daughter they had never had. They became very dear to me, as did the boys.

My spine began to bend and Mr. Eyre Brook recommended that I should have swimming lessons. It was arranged that I should go to Mayors Paddock Swimming Baths in Bristol with the physiotherapist from Winford Hospital. I had to have the afternoon off school for this and off Mum and I went by bus. Apart from the odd dip in the sea I had never been swimming. All the girls had to change in an enormous room with one small gas fire for heat. It was all very strange and archaic. When we got to the pool side we discovered that the pool was shallow at each end and deep in the middle. The boys' end was one side and the girls' the other – so in theory only the good swimmers ever met anyone of the opposite sex!

It was there that I was to meet Dennis and Ken, who have cropped up at varying times throughout my life. They were both having lessons, having suffered from polio. Most disabled people at that time had had polio and all the disabled facilites were geared for this sort of disability. I did not fit in! Mr.Gainey said that he would soon teach me to swim. Dennis swam like a fish and used to call me puffing billy as I was so sure I would go under the water that I kept dragging air into my lungs at every opportunity. Mr. Gainey tried and tried to teach me. He had never failed to teach anyone to swim, until he tried with me! It was no good, I could not stay up in the water.

Dad made me what I can only describe as some 'apparatus'. It was like a trapesium on a stand and the idea was that I would swing from my arms, thus pulling my spine straight. My arms were just not strong enough to support my weight, so Dad would hold my hands on the bar. My hands would blister and I hated the whole performance, which really did not do any good anyway!

At eleven I passed my 'eleven plus', with only three others in my class of over 30, so it meant leaving all my friends and going to the local grammar school. I was really scared, the school was enormous, the sixth formers giants, and everybody seemed to know everybody else. There was a strange anomaly that children from two schools about six miles away mainly passed their 'eleven plus' examination and only a few went to their local secondary modern school. These children filled the grammar school on my doorstep making it rare for anyone from our town to go there. After a while I settled down, made friends and enjoyed myself.

Chapter One

At 13 and a half, I had to go into Winford Orthopaedic Hospital to have my spine straightened. When I got in there I was put on what seemed like a rack. My feet were tied to one end and my neck to another, then a handle was turned and I gradually stretched. When I had gone far enough I was put in a plaster jacket. This then had to dry and that was horrible. Having a heavy, wet, cold plaster from my hips to under my chin was frightening and for a few days I was delirious and a dreadful patient. When it dried it felt better but was still uncomfortable and dug into my hips whenever I sat up. I complained and was told I was being a baby. After two weeks the first operation took place through a hole cut in the plaster. When I came around I was in the day room, with a drip and a pain in my back and pain in both hips. When the morphine wore off this was unbearable and so I screamed and screamed! I woke all the babies in the next ward so a doctor was sent for. He was not the one for my team, but eventually as I would not shut up he cut my plaster around my hip bones. For a moment there was silence and then one of the nurses pushed the mirror attached to my bed out of my reach. There was a lot of whispering and then other people came to look and finally dressings were applied. I was to find out later that the paster had been rubbing on my bony hip bones and while I was lying on my stomach for the operation, the skin had completely broken down and when it was uncovered it was black. I had to have it dressed every day for about four months.

I was in hospital for a year, but this was nothing like as bad as it sounds. The worst bit was the three operations, and being in a plaster jacket, but the rest of the time it was like a boarding school as I had to stay in hospital for my education, but could go home in the school holidays. I could not walk in my jacket as it was too heavy and my school had lots of steps so in hospital I stayed. However it was fun! The girls on D Ward used to have crushes on the porters. The porters, all young lads, were flattered at all the attention they got and used to meet us in 'Passion Alley' when we could sneak out of the ward. If they wrote to us, or brought us flowers, well that was excitement! We were always being banned from watching television for some misdemeanour or another.

While I was in hospital I got to know Mr. Eyre Brook. I had been under his care for most of my life, mostly seeing him every 3-6 months in out-patients. Up until then he had been the powerful figure, always dressed in grey, whose presence seemed to demand respect and the very idea of asking a question was unthinkable. When I passed my 'eleven plus' he was delighted, and told all the staff at the out-patient department, but still I was too scared to talk to him. At the time when I was in hospital, if a consultant did a ward round all the beds had to be tidy, whether the consultant was seeing the patient or not, there had to be silence on the ward and the patients did not speak unless spoken to. One day Mr. Eyre Brook came around with some students and started to talk about me and my operation. He got out my x-rays and held them up, but they were on an angle to me and I could not see them. I was so interested in what he was saying that I called out, 'Can I see the x-rays please – the ones before the operation and the ones afterwards?' There was silence, Sister was mortified and I knew that I was in trouble. Mr. Eyre Brook turned to me and beamed. "How lovely to find someone interested in what I am trying to do for them" he said and proceeded to go right back through my x-rays and explain everything he had done.

From that day on, we were great friends and still exchange Christmas cards to this day.

Denise followed me to the grammar school, but she had problems too. She was much taller than anyone in her year and she used to cry in her bedroom because she was so tall, while I was crying in the other because I was so small. Our poor mother!!

When I got back to school, it was hard work preparing for my 'O' levels. I managed to persuade my teachers not to keep me back a year and worked hard in catching up, until I passed 6 'O' levels, enough to get me into the 6th form. I was all set to go to University, but went off the idea and ended up at a local Technical College taking a secretarial course. I'm glad that I did. By the end of the year's course I had had enough and could not wait to get to work. I don't think I would have survived three years at university.

When I left the grammar school, the Head asked to see me and said that he had something to tell me which he felt I should know. He stuttered a bit and then said that when he first heard I had passed for the school, he told the Governors that he did not want me in the school as he felt with my disability I would be "too disruptive" to the rest of the pupils. Fortunately for me, the Governors had overruled him and said that I had to be given a term's trial to see if I could cope, and if I was not managing then I would have to go to a "Special School" as they were called in those days. The Head said that he had completely changed his mind after I had been there for a few days and he felt that I had been an asset to the school. I thought it was quite brave of him to admit all that to me.

I got the first and only job I applied for—a trainee medical secretary at Frenchay Hospital. Funnily enough, my mother had hated teaching and always wanted to work in a hospital, but 'nice girls' did not work in hospitals before the war, they went into teaching! Mum and Dad were very happy for me to work in a hospital and during the years I was there worked my way up to being in charge of the General Surgery Unit office. Denise, meanwhile had left school at 16 and gone to work at Southmead Hospital in the laboratories. Not long afterwards mum got a job in the antenatal clinic also at Southmead Hospital, so we were all in the NHS. Dad was a quarry manager at this time, and used to joke that perhaps he should go and train to be an ambulance driver.

Chapter Two

My parents attended the little Baptist church near my grandparents home – Mum and Auntie Marjorie taking it in turns to play the organ, Grampy being secretary, and treasurer, and Nanny doing the flowers. There was only an evening service here and as we moved to Chipping Sodbury when I was two, I was sent to the Baptist church there to Sunday School. I loved it. I loved singing, learning recitations, listening to the stories, meeting my friends there – everything about it. As I got older I began to realise that this was not just a nice story about a kind man who loved little children. This Jesus loved me and because of that he had left his beautiful home in heaven and come to earth to die on a cross for me. I talked this over with my friend Marion and we decided we wanted to know more. We were only 10 but decided that we wanted to give our lives to God and we wanted to be baptised. Our minister, Henry Bunday was flabbergasted and did not know what to do. We were so young, but we did seem to know what we wanted, so he went to his area superintendent, Mr Durant, and asked his advice. Mr Durant said he himself had been baptised at 9, but he agreed to meet with us and he gave us some lessons so that we understood completely what we were doing. So, in the August, when I was just 11, I was baptised. Wouldn't it be great to say that I have never looked back, that my Christian life has gone on in leaps and bounds? It would not be true.

I was not afraid, however, to say that I was a Christian and we had some lively arguments in our religious education lessons. I am one of those people who can usually think of the perfect argument a long time after the event but I can remember one particular day when the argument about life after death had been going on and on, until Pete Gezelinski said to me "Well, I feel sorry for you. When you die and find there is nothing there and that is the end, you will be really disappointed." To which I replied "If I die and there is nothing there how will I be able to feel anything, but on the other hand if you die and find there is something there, you will be the one who is disappointed."

As I got older one major thing loomed larger and ever larger in my life. Why was I small? I read an article about dwarfs being unlucky, but I did not know I was called a dwarf until whilst I was in hospital someone said to me 'I was told to look out for you, that I would easily recognise you because of you being a dwarf' I cried for three days, I did not eat and I wanted to die and I never wanted to face anyone again. Gradually, I bounced back, but always there was this feeling – why me? God did not seem to have any answers.

I started to pray for a miracle, some nights I was convinced that when I woke the next morning I would be tall, that none of my clothes would fit. But it never happened. "But I'll give all the glory to you, God" I'd cry "If only you would make me tall". Denise was 5' 10", Dad 6' 3", Mum 5' 8", why was I 3' 7"?

My cousin Terry, three years older than me and like everyone in my family very tall, was like a brother to me. He would take me out on bike rides, and every Sunday morning when we got back from church, there was Terry, sometimes with some of his friends, having cycled the three miles from his home for some of my mum's jam tarts. Mum always made a fruit tart of some sort to follow the roast on a Sunday and with the left over pastry she made jam tarts. As their fame spread and Terry brought more and more friends, so she made more and more tarts!

My grandfather had died when I was 13 and when I was 18 my grandmother was killed as she crossed the road. Just a few weeks before that I had visited her one evening and she had told me how much she missed my grandfather and how she was looking forward to going to be with him in Heaven. I was upset by her death, but I knew that she was ready to go. Terry and his parents had been living with her and he was particularly upset by her death. My best friend, Sue, who lived near me, worked in a shop close to where Terry worked on Saturdays and she was able to give him support and they started to go out together.

Mr. Eyre Brook persuaded the powers that be that I should be given an invalid car and eventually they found one that I could manage. Yet again, everything was geared for those who had had polio and no one could cope with me. They kept saying that I could not manage an invalid car, but Mr. Eyre Brook persisted. At sixteen I could at last travel under my own steam without having to pedal. That gave me independence – I even drove it to Cornwall on holiday. Gradually I got involved with the Disabled Drivers Association, and I started to have boyfriends and one thing led to another and I went to church less and less. There were often events taking place on a Sunday and I would try to go to church first, but more and more often I chose the trip with the club rather than church. My Christian friends and leaders tried to warn me about the path I was taking, but I felt accepted amongst other disabled people, sadly much more so than I did at church and the longer I did not go to church the more embarrassed I was at going at all.

At eighteen we moved house and left our council house to buy a house in nearby Yate. This house was away from the main road which, since my grandmother's death on a stretch of that same road, had terrified my mother. It was a lovely house and we settled in and got to know the neighbours in no time.

At work I was attending a college course on a day release scheme and I started to go out with boys from that course too, so my social life was full, yet empty. I did not really know any small people, if I saw somebody I would be overcome with embarrassment and look the other way. I certainly did not want to meet anyone who was small like me.

One day an Iraqi friend who was on the same course as me at college asked me if I was going to watch a programme called 'Born to be Small' which was to be broadcast. He felt I should watch it as he said that I should accept myself and he did not feel I did. I was offended and did not make any promises. When I was at home, I was aware of my mum having something on her mind and then she asked me to watch the same programme. Much against my better judgement, just to prove it really did not matter to me (when it mattered oh so much) I agreed to watch it.

I sat down with my parents, prepared for half an hour of sheer hell and embarrassment, watching all these ugly people who could not do anything, yet were like me. I was glued to the set. Here were people, alright they were small, but some were pretty, some not so pretty, some clever, some not at all bright, some funny, some rather pitiful – just like any other cross section of the public. At last I knew what God had been telling me for years. I was just an ordinary person, small maybe, but I was me. Out there in the big wide world were lots of people who looked like me, but they were ordinary too. I could not believe it. Dad said 'Well, what did you think.' I said, ' Some of those girls are really pretty' and Dad turned to me and said straight away, 'You're really pretty'. Up until that moment I had thought I was one of the ugliest people in the world! Lots of people said to me that I had lovely eyes, but I always thought they meant that the rest of me was so ugly.

Everything fell into place. I felt ordinary – there were other people like me. When I went to work the next day everyone noticed the difference. Before watching that film if I had a dream about myself I was always tall. Since that night, in my dreams I have always been small.

At the end of the film they mentioned an organisation for people of restricted growth and I could not wait to join. I found out there were three more girls in the Bristol area and two of us travelled up to London to the next meeting early in March. We were met at the station by Mary Lindsey – at that time sub-editor of the scientific journal Nature. She took us back to her car – a mini which had been specially adapted for her. I was fascinated. I had been to the Ministry of Health in Bristol asking for advice on having a car adapted and had been told I would have to have hand controls. As my hands are small, I did not feel that this was the answer; I could use my legs perfectly well, they just would not reach the pedals. Mary had her pedals lengthened, her seat raised and was able to weave her way in and out of the London traffic with ease.

We went to the meeting and there were lots and lots of people like us! It was amazing. I could actually walk up to someone and start a conversation, looking them in the face, without having to attract their attention from a position below their waist. It was a real eye opener to me.

May and I returned to Bristol determined to meet up with the other two girls we had been told about and this we did. When one goes anywhere on one's own and is stared at it can be embarrassing, but when there is more than one it is hilarious and the tables are really turned. We had great fun meeting together in Bristol and then going to every meeting of the Association we could wherever it was held.

The first thing I did when I got back to Bristol was to go to the nearest Mini dealer and buy a new Mini Automatic, which the garage adapted for me. I had a fantastic driving instructor, who I chose from random from the telephone book, but we got on well together and I soon took my test and passed. I felt that the sky was the limit.

The Chairman of the Association at that time, Charles Pocock, soon roped me in to be Secretary as the person who had been Secretary for some time was wanting to relinquish the post. With my mini I could easily travel up to London for the committee meetings and life became exciting.

One weekend my parents arranged to go to London to hear the London Emmanuel Choir in the evening. The coach fare was one pound, cheap even in those days. The idea was that people would have the afternoon free and go to hear the choir in the evening. As luck would have it, there was an Association meeting that afternoon, so I thought I would go up by coach, go to my meeting and then meet up with my parents for the evening. My parents had not decided what to do in the afternoon, so I suggested they came with me to my meeting. They had not thought of that and then Mum said she would feel out of place as everyone would be small. I said that I had felt out of place in this world all my life as everyone was tall. They decided to go with me, and thoroughly enjoyed themselves. They said if only they had been able to go to such a meeting when they first knew about me, all their worries would have disappeared. They were so happy to see so many people like me and what with that and a lovely evening at the Central Hall, it truly was a day to remember.

In all this excitement I did not forget God. Not immediately, but bit by bit I went back to Him. Our church was without a minister and my parents had been going to the Baptist church in Horfield to hear the minister Arthur Liston. I started to go with them and under his leadership, and with my new found knowledge about myself, I again found the One who gives purpose to every life, if only we are not too blind to see it.

Chapter Three

Life was going really well for me. I was happy at work and at play! I was taking a college course to become a medical records officer, and I had decided that I did not want any serious relationships. I had a few admirers and lots of friends. I was going places and I really wallowed in my new found self-confidence.

One weekend May, one of the girls from Bristol, and I went to a dinner dance near London. The arrangement was that we would stay the night with her sister in Romford. After the dance, feeling very tired and with May saying she knew exactly where her sister lived we set off- only to find ourselves nearly in Southend. We turned round and started back to London, when there was an awful noise in the engine and I slammed on the brakes. My mini was only six months old, yet a con rod had come off the engine and smashed the gear box and the engine. We tried to call out the AA but could not get through and eventually called the Police who kindly took us to May's sister. Meanwhile my mini had to be towed to Southend for repair. We travelled back to Bristol the following day by coach and I was carless for several weeks.

As Secretary of the Association for Research into Restricted Growth I had to arrange the Christmas dinner dance in London and this I did. All sorts of people phoned me with enquiries about the Association and I was kept busy answering their queries.

At last my car was ready for collection and I had to travel to Southend. As the car had a new engine and I would have to drive slowly I arranged to stay with my Cornish cousin Graham who was in the RAF and stationed with his wife at RAF Brize Norton. The journey back was boring and I was glad when I reached Brize Norton. Graham went with me to the phone box to phone home and say I had arrived safely. When you are my height, it is very difficult to open the doors of phone boxes and to actually reach the phone is impossible. Mum was relieved that I had got that far, and mentioned that I had had a call from a Mr. Phillips from Suffolk and he would be phoning back on Monday evening. Silly as it might seem, I knew then that this was important.

On the dot of seven o'clock on Monday evening, the phone rang. It was Mr. Phillips who said that he had written to the Chairman about joining the Association and wanted tickets for the dinner dance. He also wanted to know where he could stay in London on the night of the dance. I told him that four of us from Bristol were staying at the Hotel where the event was being held, and offered to book a room for him when I confirmed our booking.

On the following Sunday I got ready for church and was just about to leave when I had a feeling that he would be phoning so I stayed home. Sure enough, he phoned again and asked me to meet him at the hotel for a coffee when I arrived.

The day of the dance dawned . Rosemary had elected to drive us to London this time and I was navigating; a big mistake! We got lost in London and were very late arriving at the Hotel. I was met with the message to contact Mr. Phillips and given his room number. We were shown to our rooms, which were all in different parts of the Hotel. Rosemary and Rosalie on one floor and May and I on another, but not in adjoining rooms. We came to my room first and I went in, had a sudden thought that I did not know where May was, and rushed from the room hoping to see her disappearing into her room. The door slammed behind me and I was left in a long corridor with doors closed on all sides of me. I knew I could not reach the lift buttons so it was no good going back to the lift and I had no idea where the stairs were. I went up to several doors and whispered 'May' as loudly as I dared, but no one answered me.

I was just beginning to panic when I saw a fellow walking down the corridor towards me. "Miss Bonney?" he said. "Mr. Phillips?" I replied "I've locked myself out of my room." He told me to call him Vic and took me back to his room to phone for a porter who came and let me in. When we were walking down the corridor I had the strangest desire to catch hold of his hand. We were too late for our promised coffee, so we went to our rooms and changed for the evening. Vic and I spent all the evening together. He told me that on the phone I sounded like someone who wore horn-rimmed glasses and thick stocking and brogues. He had asked me for a coffee so that I could introduce him to a nice young girl! However, that night he decided that he did not want to be introduced to anyone else, ever, and asked me to marry him. I accepted.

Most people thought I was mad. Vic was 17 years older than me at 42. He was a welder and lived in Suffolk. I just knew that this was God's plan for me. I returned home on the Sunday with Vic's signet ring on my chain round my neck, until he could get me an engagement ring. My parents thought I had taken leave of my senses and really did not take me seriously. However, Vic phoned me every night and I wrote to him every day. We made arrangements for him to come to stay over the New Year and this is when we officially got engaged. Mum and Dad liked Vic straight away and Mum said to me "I wish Vic was not so much older than you, but you will never find anyone who loves you as much as he does."

One of the first things we did was to go to church. Arthur Liston was delighted at our news and promised to marry us. Vic had never been to church unless it was for a special occasion, but he happily went along with me each time he came down. We went out in my car one night and made our marriage vows to each other and before God and they felt as binding as if we had been married in a church.

When I went back to work wearing my engagement ring everyone was astounded, but on hearing that Vic was a welder, one of the nursing sisters said her husband's friend owned a welding firm and they arranged an interview for Vic. My friend Angela had an aunt who had turned part of her house into a bed sit, so everything fell into place for Vic to move down to the West Country. Every few weeks Vic either came down to Yate, or I went to Suffolk or we met in London, until the Easter when I went to Suffolk and loaded my car up with Vic's things, he loaded his car up and left his home for good. His elderly parents were pleased that at last he had found someone to love, but they were sorry to see him leave as he had in many ways been their lifeline.

Chapter Four

Vic had come from an "Army family". His father had been in the Royal Engineers, Mounted Section, and his two brothers and sister had followed. Vic's arrival had been a shock to the family. His mother had been told to take him home, put him in a corner and forget him as he would never be any good! One aunt had disowned the family as they had brought disgrace upon the family name by having a son like Vic. However, he had other aunts who thought a lot of him, especially his father's sister Aunt Tuss.

Vic's parents had brought him up to be independent, sending him to local schools, but he had always preferred to be alone and spent a lot of time with his animals, dogs and horses. He had become an expert poacher – both for game and fish! During the war he had caught so many rabbits that at one time he was earning more money than his father. When he left school his father apprenticed him to a black-smith and he learned to weld. Still, he felt that he was letting the family down because he could not get into the Army and he pestered the enlistment office to let him in, but even in the sections dealing with animals where height was not so crucial, they would not let him in. At 18 he was contacted by someone who worked for Billy Smart's Circus and he decided that he would leave home and join them.

He stayed there for ten years and always says that the education he received there was better than that at any university or college. He met people from all over the world, learned smatterings of their language, their culture, their way of cooking. He was mainly a clown, learning all the old slapstick tricks which have thrilled circus crowds for years. He worked with some of the great names in the circus world and had lots of fun. It was hard work and sometimes dangerous. He often clowned from horseback and had a few nasty falls, but he loved it. He travelled all over this country, but never went abroad. His main love was the animals. He had a pet monkey who was adept at finding things lost in the big top, and on one occasion found an engagement ring, much to the relief of the owner. He was friends with the elephants too. He would often ride an elephant and use her to help raise the big top. His favourite was Burma, and when he saw her about 15 years later he called her the pet name he had always used Burmeska, and she recognised him immediately. Elephants don't forget! One unforgettable night he held a lioness whilst she had an emergency Caesarean Section and she died in his lap.

At the end of each season Vic, in company with other performers would go to whoever would pay the most for the next season, and in this way he worked with Chipperfields, Billy Smart, and Bertram Mills. Billy Smart was a favourite employer. He was strict but fair and would always insist that the animals were made comfortable, fed and watered before the human performers were allowed to look after themselves.

The first year he was in circus Vic was in the Christmas Show at Harringay Arena where he met Princess Margaret.

Vic had to learn to sew, iron, cook and generally look after himself whilst he was in circus. Skills, which I have always been grateful for in him!

Eventually, after ten years, Vic decided he had had enough. The day of the circus was dying. He left the circus and went to work as a welder. He had several good friends, but the majority of his time was spent with his horses. When he was a boy he had one called Cobber. Vic would whistle him from his bedroom window and then climb down on to his back to go out for a night ride, unbeknown to his parents! He also spent time fishing and shooting, usually illegally, and when I met him he had an Alsation dog which was trained to the gun. He had five ponies when we met, but he sold three and brought just the two down with him.

We found a field for these two horses, but it proved to be a very expensive hobby. In Suffolk, land was cheap but around Bristol it was much dearer, and not so easily available, so we had to travel quite a way to see the ponies. These two, Hondas and Ajax, were unbroken and we finally made the decision to sell them as they were a big financial liability. The father of a friend bought them and they were well looked after. Hondas was the proud one, the aristocrat, whilst Ajax, my favourite, was rather like a donkey! When the time came for them to go in the horse box, Vic said that

Ajax would be a problem, but that Hondas was always well behaved. I held Ajax by his halter and told him about the new field he was going to, how there was a stream running through it and another pony already there waiting for him. I was thoroughly laughed at by both Vic and my friend's father, but Ajax walked up the ramp into the horse box immediately he was asked. Hondas was another story. Two hours later, he still would not get in the box! Even Ajax was getting impatient and was turning round to him and telling him off. Eventually, Hondas was boxed and off they went to their new home. We missed them, but really we did not have the facilities to look after them properly.

Vic enjoyed his new job and on his first day made friends with Alan, who was also new to the firm – a friendship which has grown and has included Alan's wife Shirley for the past 22 years.

We set our wedding date for the 10th November and started to make all the plans. About this time my sister, Denise, met a boy called Terry. He was 6'4" with a big black beard. From the first we all loved him dearly. He was full of fun and we were all so pleased when they got engaged just before our wedding.

Rosemary and Rosalie had agreed to be my bridesmaids, May was too shy. They wore white dresses with purple velvet cloaks with hoods edged in fur. My dress had a lace hood. It was a lovely day – I think it rained, but it did not matter. Vic's best friend from Suffolk, David, was best man and many of my Cornish relative came up for the occasion.

Vic and I went to Devon for a few days honeymoon and then back to a flat in Clifton, Bristol. Vic and I had been determined to buy a house, but our finances were such that it would be difficult, and the only houses we could afford were not in a very nice area. Mum advised us to approach our local council to see if they would help us. We were not too keen at first as we wanted to own our own house, but we did approach them, and as events proved it could well have been disastrous if we hadn't. They agreed that in the flats they were building they would build one especially for us, with the kitchen, etc. at our level. However, that was not ready so we had to rent another flat and the only one we could get was a damp, mice infested hovel, but we were very happy there for just over a year until our flat was finished.

At last we moved into our flat in Chipping Sodbury. It felt like a palace. It had two bedrooms, a spacious lounge and kitchen, bathroom and toilet – all of which was on our level. We loved entertaining.

Prior to this we had been attending Horfield Baptist Church with Arthur Liston but coinciding with our move to Chipping Sodbury, some 10 miles from the church, Arthur told the church that he was leaving as he had been appointed Area Superintendent for the North East. While he was talking to us about getting married he had asked us our views on having children. This is not an easy decision when you are disabled with a disease which is hereditary. However much you want children, is it fair to bring them into the world when you are pretty sure they will be similarly affected? We prayed about it together with Arthur and we all felt that if God wanted us to have children then we would have them. If not, nothing would happen.

Just before Arthur left the area he came out with his wife one evening and we spent a time in prayer asking God's direction in the matter of children.

We knew that living so far from Horfield it would be difficult to get there to any midweek meetings and we felt we should go back to the church where I was baptised and this we did and settled in happily there with the minister Sam Highway. We talked and prayed with him about whether or not we should have children, and the answer always seemed to be the same – leave it to God. So we did and early in February 1976 I discovered that I was pregnant. We were thrilled. My parents were horrified! They had known such pain when I was stared at, when I had to have operations, when I had had disappointments, that they just did not want me to go through all that too. Denise was thrilled, she was married to Terry by then and they were both excited at the prospect of having a niece or nephew. Denise talked to Mum and Dad and soon Mum at least got excited at the prospect of a grandchild and started knitting like mad!

The baby was expected in September and I was to have a Caesarean section. All progressed smoothly and I had no raised blood pressure, back ache or anything which other people have. I felt really well. The arthritis which attacks my loose joints disappeared and I blossomed.

At the end of May we went to Cornwall and stayed with Auntie Florrie and Uncle Demps for a week. The night before we went the baby had been quiet and had not kicked. I was beginning to get worried, but Vic kept reassuring me that everything was alright. We started off to Cornwall in the early hours of the morning, to avoid the heavy traffic. Just when we went over the River Tamar, the baby gave a hefty kick and did not stop for the rest of the holiday. The kicking even managed to spill a cup of tea I was holding one day.

Vic had taken his welding plant and spent a great deal of the holiday welding up gates, etc. on the smallholding. I enjoyed spending time with Auntie Florrie. At the bottom of the lane by her house was a small hut in which the ladies of the area used to meet and hold whist drives, Tupperware parties, etc. and she asked me to go to the next whist drive the following night. That night Vic went up to bed and forgot to take out his plate with his false tooth on it in the bathroom, so he took it out upstairs and wrapped it in his handkerchief and put it in his trouser pocket. Next morning he put on his trousers, sat down and broke his plate. For the rest of the holidays he had to go around with a gap in his front teeth. That evening I went to the whist drive and was surprised when I won a prize. The prizes were only fun items – and my prize was a pair of sweet false teeth! We did laugh. All too soon our holiday was over and we returned home.

Then in June a big lump appeared at the side of my stomach. As the day wore on it began to hurt until I could not bear any clothes to touch it and could hardly move. I was admitted to hospital and immediately taken to the operating theatre. They opened me up but found that it was an enormous fibroid, and as it was actually in the womb they could do nothing about it, but that it would subside naturally. That summer was one of the hottest on record and my room was unbearable. Mum had bought an electric fan when she was expecting Denise and she brought that in. It used to stay on day and night, only going off to cool down now and then. My room was the coolest on the floor. Of course the worry then was that having been through surgery I would go into premature labour and lose the baby, but there was absolutely no sign of that. They used to listen to the baby's heart beat every few hours and one evening they did that while my father was visiting. He did not want to hear it, he was still very unhappy about me having a baby and he went off for a walk so he would miss it – but the nurse waited until he came back! He was so excited that he went home and stayed out in the road washing his car for ages just so that he could tell everyone who passed "I've just heard my grandchild's heartbeat!"

I soon went home and got larger and larger, until I was 42 and a half inches round and the same tall. Mum and Dad were almost as excited as us at the prospect of the baby and used to insist that I had to eat fresh vegetables by the lorryload it seemed, for the sake of the baby.

At last my obstetrician gave me a date. She wanted to perform the Caesarean on 22nd September. She assured me that as the baby would be quite small and would have to go into the special care baby unit for a while, they would get it back to me as soon as possible so that it did not get used to anyone else lifting it. Vic came into hospital with me and went down to wait outside the theatre. He could not believe it when the doctor came out with a 6 lb. 4 oz. baby girl, with her eyes wide open. There was no question of her going into special care and she came back to my side room with me. The obstetrician had felt it best for me to be on my own so that I learned to cope in the best way possible for me, which would not necessarily be the way other people did it. When I came round from the anaesthetic I did not believe she was ours and said to Vic that they must have made a mistake.

She was so beautiful. We called her Emma Bonney Phillips and I doubt if there have ever been any prouder parents, grandparents or aunt and uncle. Terry had always said he wanted me to have a girl as he had always had a desire to make a dolls house. He was so talented with his hands and I knew Emma would have a dolls house to be proud of.

All through my pregnancy I had been intending to write to Arthur Liston, but time went on and I didn't, so it seemed more sensible to write with the news of the baby's arrival. However, just two weeks before her birth, we were saddened to read that he had died suddenly of a heart attack. He was just the same age as Vic. I wrote to his wife and she said how thrilled he would have been at Emma's arrival, but as we all knew, by that time he was with his Lord and knew all about Emma anyway.

The paediatricians assured me that Emma was normal, but I did not believe them and said that I had not been diagnosed until I was two. They X-rayed Emma and thrust the X-rays at me saying they were normal and there was no way they could change. I was really upset as I had been prepared to wait to see if there was anything wrong, and I felt sure that they did not really understand what they were talking about.

I went home after about 8 days. Emma was slightly jaundiced and slow to feed, but eventually we settled into a routine. However, I did not understand her and I got into a panic each time she cried. It always seemed as if my mum or my sister could get her off to sleep, or stop her crying, but I never could. It seemed to get worse until Mothers' Day when we were all at my mother's house and Emma started to cry. I did not even try to pick her up as I knew she would not stop for me. Mum tried, Denise tried, Dad tried, Vic tried and in desperation they gave her to me. She looked up at me, gave a big sigh, beamed at me and stopped crying. What a Mothers' Day present! That seemed to be the start of an understanding which brought us closer.

I might not have managed to do things the way others did, but Emma thrived and began to talk at about nine months and walked on her first birthday. The paediatrician kept telling me at her check-ups that she was normal, yet she was not as big as other babies born at the same time, she certainly had much smaller feet, and what was very signifi- cant to me and my mum was that she had fat thumb nails. I kept going to my GP with my worries and he really did not know the answers. He, a non-Christian, said to me whatever Emma was like not to let anyone ever tell me she should not be here. He said if she was not meant to be here I would have lost her either early on, or at least when I had my fibroid, so Emma was definitely meant to be here.

I did not know what I wanted. Did I want Emma to be tall or small? I only had experience of being small and I enjoyed life. Did tall people enjoy life as much? It was difficult to leave it all in God's hands. I did what I am so good at – gave it to God with one hand and took it back with the other.

Our minister, Sam Highway, knew that I had a tendency to be depressed, so he encouraged a few mums in the church to start a Toddler at Two club which over the years has grown and grown. At one of the first meetings I met a new mum to the area, Trish and her son Steven, and that started a friendship which is still going strong.

I began to really enjoy Emma. She chatted non-stop and had lots of common sense. She blossomed on all the love she was shown, but did not become precocious. Although Vic was older than most dads he had all the time in the world for her and loved to bath her, change her, sing to her, play with her, nothing was too much trouble for her.

Unfortunately, our neighbours in the flat had lots of problems and began to make our lives a misery – imitating the way I walked, making fun of us, shouting at Emma to shut up if she was chatting to me while I was putting out the washing, as well as shouting and swearing at each other at all hours of the day and night. We asked the council if we could move and they agreed. Other people had complained about our neighbours and they were very sympathetic. However, they said they would have to move us to a two bedroomed house, they could not move us to another flat. Vic and I talked about this and thought that if we had to move to a house, we might as well have another baby and move to a three bedroomed house. We finally decided on Emma's birthday that we would definitely try for another baby. Within six weeks I knew I was pregnant again.

This time Mum and Dad were more pleased and mum started to knit again. Christmas came and this year it was not so good. Terry and Denise had awful colds which seemed to go on and on and they obviously were not well. Terry seemed depressed and Denise said that he had had a big shock. An elderly man at work often asked Terry to work on his car and Terry helped whenever he could. Just before Christmas he asked Terry to change a fan belt. Terry said he would do it later, but that lunch hour he was going to the pub as the boss was buying all the men a drink. Terry ate his lunch in the canteen and as he walked across the car park he found the man dead by his car. He was frantic and tried mouth-to-mouth resuscitation, but to no avail. In fact the man had not even lifted the bonnet on his car, but Terry blamed himself for his death and had become quite obsessed with it.

Terry had told me when we were talking one day that he was a twin, his twin being miscarried. As my twin had been still-born, I felt an affinity with Terry and really thought of him like the brother I had never had. I felt sure Terry would bounce back from this shock and did not worry too much.

Chapter Five

That winter was snowy and miserable. Denise and Terry had colds, we had colds, I was pregnant and got tired easily. It seemed just when I needed a sleep in the afternoons, Emma dispensed with hers. What with one thing and another we did not see much of Terry and Denise. They were not on the phone at home and if I needed to get in touch with her it had to be at work, so I only did that in an emergency. They saw Mum and Dad and messages were passed on.

One Sunday afternoon we called over to see them and Emma had a plastic figure of Kermit the frog which Terry with his big hands magically kept turning into a walnut! Emma was fascinated and could not understand how it was done. Terry and Denise kept goats and Emma loved to go over there to visit them. They had chickens, rabbits, a pheasant and cats – a child's paradise. While we were over there Denise was asking Emma if she would like to go and stay with them sometime. Emma was a little uncertain. She had only ever stayed with Grannie, but she thought she might.

One Friday morning I went round to Mum's and thought I saw Denise driving away – Mum made some excuse and I did not think any more of it. Mum and Dad had Emma for the Saturday night while Vic and I went to an Association meeting in London. We came back on the Sunday and collected Emma.

On the Wednesday, Valentine's Day, I had an antenatal appointment. We had arranged for my friend Jackie to have Emma while we went to the hospital and we were just leaving the house when the phone rang. It was my dad and he simply said "We have lost our Terry" I did not understand what he meant at first and then it hit me, Terry was dead. Dad could not say any more than that Denise wanted me to keep my appointment and then go round to her. Terry always rode a motor bike to work and I assumed that he must have had an accident.

Vic drove me to Jackie's and she agreed to keep Emma as long as necessary and we went off to the hospital. I could not stop crying and Vic had to go in and explain what had happened and ask that I could be seen straight away. We went straight back to Denise's house where Mum and Dad, and Terry's brother Dave and his wife Elaine were. The story they told was too horrible to understand and take in.

Terry had been depressed since Christmas and the week before he had said to Denise that he was not sure whether he wanted to stay with her, he could not think straight about anything. After the death of his friend at work, he had been passed over for a promotion and this had played on his mind.

On 9th February he had gone to stay with his mother for the weekend so that he could sort himself out. On the Monday, he had gone back to Denise and said that he felt his uncertainties were all due to depression. He would go to the doctor the next day and at the weekend he would go and get the wood and start on Emma's dolls house. He thought he would feel better if he could get stuck into a project like that. He took Denise out for a meal to celebrate.

The next day Denise had gone off to work as usual, leaving Terry to go to the doctor. When she got home at night there was a note saying he could not go on, with the words Deer Park written at the bottom of the note. His shotgun was missing. She did not know what to do. Firstly she phoned the police who said it was a domestic matter and they could do nothing. Then she drove to Gloucester to get Terry's brother Dave and his wife and then phoned Dad as she knew he would just have got home from work. They then all went to the Deer Park in Berkeley. Snow was on the ground and it was freezing cold. With their small torches they tried to search but the area was so vast they could not find him. Dad then went into a cottage on the edge of the park and the people there said they had heard a gun shot. Dad phoned the police again and insisted that they come. This time they came, with large floodlights. It was Dave who found his brother's body.

The police said that they could not take the body back that night, it would have to wait until the morning, as they did not have a suitable vehicle. Dave could not bear the thought of Terry lying there all night and asked the owner of the cottage if he could borrow his landrover. He was thus able to bring his brother's body back.

Apparently when Terry had gone to the doctor he was told that he should pull himself together and that there was nothing wrong with him.

I cannot begin to put across the horror of that day. Inside my brain I could hear a voice repeating "Suicides are buried outside the walls of the city". I could hardly bear to look at the despair on Denise's face. Her complete bewilderment, her sense of betrayal, broke my heart. Mum and Dad had loved him like a son and could not understand why he had not talked to them. Where had they failed him, where had they fallen short that he did not feel able to approach them? Dave and Elaine, Vic and I were all asking the same questions.

As we left Denise to go to fetch Emma, I felt I would never rest again as this voice kept repeating itself in my head. When we went through Chipping Sodbury I could see the lights were on in the church study so we went in to see Sam Highway. He managed to make some sense of the situation for me. He said that depression was an illness. Like cancer, some people had treatment and recovered completely, some had treatment and did not recover, some people did not realise how bad they were. Suicide was often the end result of untreated depression, or depression which did not respond to treatment and should be treated like the fatal result of any illness. This helped me a great deal and stilled the insistent voice inside my head. Sam also said that he would be available to Denise at any time if she wanted to talk to him.

As the days went on it seemed as if his death and the manner of it affected everyone who had ever had any knowledge of him. We all felt we had failed him. People he worked with called, old friends, relations, they all said the same thing. We spent as much time with Denise as possible, but the family decided that as I was pregnant I should not go to Terry's funeral, so I was not there with her. I found it very difficult to accept that Terry had gone and I think the fact that I did not go to the funeral contributed to this. A friend said that I was taking it too hard "after all he was only your brother-in-law". I was very upset by this comment, but Mum said perhaps they did not realise that in our family we forgot the 'in law' bit of any relationship.

I will never forget how brave my sister was. She refused to drive for a few days as she said she was not safe, but then she got on with her life. She went to see a psychiatrist who helped to explain the way in which Terry's personality showed that he was a potential suicide risk—his highs were too high and his lows too low. One day Denise felt she could not go on and in desperation remembered Sam Highway's offer to talk to her, so she phoned him from work and made arrangements to go to see him. Her department at South-mead were so good to her, they did all they could to help her. She had several meetings with Sam and felt better for them.

Six weeks after Terry's death, Vic got up as usual and went to work. I got up, got Emma up and dressed, got out some lamb chops to defrost for dinner that evening and let in my home help. She was cleaning around when I looked up and in walked Vic and my doctor, Steve Gregson. I went cold—I knew it was Denise. At first I thought she must have done the same as Terry, but Steve explained that she had been killed in a car crash.

The night before she had been going home from work and either Denise or the other driver had swerved to avoid a dog. Denise was fatally injured and died three hours later in hospital. Her next door neighbour had seen the car as he travelled home and thought it was one like Denise's but never dreamed it could have been hers. When the police came to ask him for her next of kin just after six o'clock he offered to phone Mum and Dad but they would not let him and said it was their responsibility.

At about 8 o'clock he thought he would phone to say he had milked Denise's goats and fed the animals, so that we could all just concentrate on Denise. When he started to talk to Mum he realised that she had no idea what he was talking about as the police still had not contacted her. He remembered the police saying she had been taken to Frenchay Hospital, so he told Mum that. Mum and Dad phoned Frenchay and were told to go down straight away. They got there as she died. Mr. May, one of the general surgeons I had worked for, had operated to try to save her, but her internal injuries were too great.

Frenchay had advised Mum and Dad to let me have a night's sleep before telling me because of my pregnancy, so Dad had met Vic when he called into the paper shop for his paper early the following morning and taken him home to break the news to him. Frenchay had also told them to get the doctor to break the news to me, hence Dr. Gregson's early morning call on me. The doctor said that if I should threaten to miscarry, I should call him and he would drive me into the hospital as neither Dad nor Vic were in a fit state to drive me, and he left phone numbers where he could be reached for the rest of the day.

Chapter Five

My poor Emma – she had had a crying mother for weeks who was just beginning to stop and then she started again. I had severe depression and did not want to get out of bed or eat, but when I thought of Emma I realised how my parents must be feeling at the loss of their daughter and I gradually began to pull myself together.

Sam Highway was able to reassure us after his talks with Denise, that he was quite sure that she was with her Lord and I felt peace in the knowledge that she now understood Terry's action as I knew that she would never have understood in this life.

This time I insisted on going to the funeral and for me the service was for both Terry and Denise. Terry's ashes had been scattered at Gloucester, near his family, but Dad had Denise's ashes brought back to our graveyeard in Chipping Sodbury.

Mum gained comfort in the thought of the coming baby and Dad in his relationship with Emma. At that time she was 2years and 7 months. One day when Dad came over she sat on his lap for about an hour (Emma never sat still on anyone's lap for long) and when he had gone she gave a sigh and said 'Grampy is still upset about Aunty Nees, isn't he?" even though not one word had been said to that effect. She was, and still is, very perceptive.

At this time Vic was suffering from severe back pain and his left leg kept going numb. He had been going for tests and it was recommended that he should go to the pain clinic for treatment. Vic's spine had been damaged through the ten years he spent in circus, mainly from several nasty falls from horses. His heavy engineering job also added to the strain.

About six weeks after Denise's death there was a front page article in the local press about a cleaner who worked where Terry had worked and had seen a ghostly hand. Insinuations were made about some supernatural power behind the two deaths. We were furious, and so were many of our friends. Lots of people phoned to complain and the paper's switchboard was jammed. It amazed us that such rubbish, which was so hurtful and had no basis, could be published.

Six weeks on again, our son Nathan was born. He looked just like Emma had done. I had wanted a girl first and had got my way and a boy second and that wish had been granted me too. Nathan weighed 6 lb. 10 oz. and was allowed home after 8 days. We hoped that this would be the start of the rebuilding of our shattered lives – but it was not to be.

Chapter Six

Sadly the treatment that Vic had at the pain clinic did not help and his pain and numbness increased. On two occasions he came in from work and collapsed with the pain in the hallway. Obviously he could not go on like that. He was referred to a neurosurgeon, Brian Cummings.

It became very obvious that the only thing which could help Vic was an operation. He was not able to work any overtime and money was tight. We worked out that we could survive if he was off work completely for up to three months – after that we would be in trouble. It was at this time too that Emma began to have problems with constipation – a direct result of the stress she had been under with the loss of Terry and Denise. Just after Christmas 1979 Emma had an X-ray of her bowel and then there was a lot of whispering and a request for more X-rays of her back and legs. Immediately I knew what they suspected – that she had inherited pseudoachondroplasia from me. I could have told them that two years before – in fact I did, but was told in no uncertain terms that I was wrong. Luckily, the consultant that Emma was under was away and there was a locum for a year. When he had the results of the X-rays he called me in and told me what I knew. It was such a relief – it explained the way she walked, her size, all the things which worried me and it was obvious that Nathan was the same. The paediatrician asked if I had any worries and I said only that when she was older she might wish I had never had her. He replied she would not be a normal teenager if she did not wish that, as they all did whether they had anything wrong or not. He said he never would have advised me not to have children.

The following day he phoned me at home to see what Vic had said as he had not come to the hospital with me. In fact Vic had said – "Good, then I won't look out of place when I take her up the aisle at her wedding". I told him this and he said he was returning to Australia at the end of the week, but that he had very much enjoyed meeting us and wished us well.

Vic went into hospital early in January for his operation; by this time he was in so much pain there was no option. When they operated they found his spinal cord was so compressed by his spinal column that in order to free it they had to damage nerves and Vic never walked unaided again. He had lots of physiotherapy and tried so hard, but he could not walk without crutches, or maybe two sticks on a good day. At the end of the three months his firm granted him redundancy as it was obvious he could not work there again. In fact he has never worked since. Although the pain was slightly better it never disappeared and Vic got very frustrated at his lack of mobility and his pain. Life seemed very bleak, but we kept going.

Mum and Dad felt that the children should have a pet. As children we had had a much loved cat called Binkie who died aged 18 years old, just after we got married. Binkie had been great company, and Vic and I would have liked to have had another cat, but although our flat was on a quiet road, there was a very busy road behind us and we would have been worried for its safety. Denise had kept tortoises when she was a child, so Mum and Dad decided to get one and keep it at their house. They promised Emma that they would get one and were horrified when they went to buy it as they were so expensive. Then he turned out to be a real escape artist and it cost them a fortune to fence him in safely! Vic chose the name – Shelly. I think probably Shelly was one of the last to be imported to this country as by the next year there was an import ban on tortoises.

We obviously could not move to a house as we had planned as Vic would not have managed the stairs comfortably, so the council said they would work something out. One day when Nathan was 14 months old, a lady who worked for the council and lived a few doors down from us, called in on her way to work to tell us about a house at Codrington, a small hamlet a few miles from Chipping Sodbury. In fact, my great grandfather had lived in Codrington and my grandmother had been brought up there. This house had previously been tenanted by a couple with a daughter in a wheelchair and it already had a lift installed. Immediately Vic said, "We'll take it" but I wanted to see it first.

Mum came with us and as we walked up the front path I knew I wanted to live there. We had the key to look around and I could visualise all my furniture placed in the rooms, how I would like the garden, and I could not wait to return the key and tell the housing manager that we would have it. We had to be back at the Housing offices by 5.00 p.m. I took the key in and said we would like it. The housing officer had become quite a friend during the months we had been wanting to move and sympathised with us in our problem with the neighbour. He said he would do his best, but there were other people who wanted the property and we would have to wait and see. I lay awake all night, planning colour schemes for each room, placing my furniture, landscaping the garden, all the time telling myself not to get to enthusiastic as we might not get the house.

The next day a letter arrived, postmarked 3.00 p.m., offering us the house. He had been teasing me all along! It took a while for the council to arrange to transfer our kitchen, but eventually we moved. Dad arranged for us to have the front dug out into a drive so that we could take the car off the road and he bought us a garage. We were so happy to have such a beautiful place. We were surrounded by fields and wildlife. We thanked God for our troublesome neighbour who had forced our move and in so doing enabled us to have Nathan.

Chapter Seven

Vic was still unable to work and although the three months had become over a year, we were still managing financially, but only just. We enjoyed pottering about in our garden and Dad was always willing to help. It was lovely for the children to have somewhere to play in safety, but I was very depressed, more so than I or anyone else realised. I had had two bereavements, a baby, a husband suddenly severely disabled and a house move, yet I felt, as a Christian, I should be coping. One day when Vic was out, the children were being difficult and I felt I just wanted to sleep, so I took about six paracetamol and lay down on the bed. All of a sudden I realised what I had done and phoned Vic. He came rushing home and made me vomit. His friend Alan and his wife Shirley were very concerned and made me promise to see my doctor. Life seemed to stretch out in front of me, never able to do anything because we had no money. I felt the children were being deprived of things which other children had. We always had to think about whether we could afford even the most basic things and I used to wake in a panic at night worrying about bills which might come. I had not really slept well since Terry had died, and I was trying to cope on 2-3 hours sleep a night. On top of all this, I felt guilty for feeling like this – I was a Christian, so shouldn't I enjoy suffering?

When I saw Steve, my G.P., he of course knew all about our family problems and said that really I should get away from home one day a week, leaving Vic to cope with the children, and I should forget home and enjoy myself. Well, we used to have to work out if we had enough money for petrol to get to Tesco, let alone for me to go off for the day, so that was a non-starter! Steve gave me something to help my depression and asked me to go back in a week.

It was about this time that I heard a sermon and it really struck me that I was the daughter of the King, and He would not let me and my family down. I stopped panicking about money and began to sleep better. Vic had to go to Frenchay Hospital for a check up, so while I was there I took the opportunity to ask if they ever wanted relief typists – I knew medical terminology from my days as a medical secretary. However, the hospital was short of money and said they rarely had funds to pay for relief typists but they would put my name down. I had asked more as a token gesture, I did not really have the confidence to go back to work anyway.

The next week I went back to see Steve and he asked what I had done about getting away from the family. I said I had put my name down at Frenchay as a relief typist and to my amazement, he clutched his head and said "I am an idiot, I am an idiot". I stared at him dumbfounded, and then he said "I had forgotten you used to be a medical secretary – would you like to work for me to cover Wendy (the practice secretary) when she is off?" I could not believe it – I was so thrilled. As I got home the phone was ringing and it was Wendy – "Steve says you will do my job when I am off, is that right? Good, I'm off next week – can you cover?" I went in to see how things were done before the end of the week and Wendy was really pleased that I would be covering her work. Usually it had to wait for her return and she was always worried that something important would be over-looked.

The next week I went over to the practice and started work along the corridor in the typing room. Everyone was very kind and said "come up and ask when you want anything". Wendy had shown me all I needed to know and when I started to listen to the tapes which the doctors had dictated, the medical terms came back to me and I merrily typed away all morning. I thoroughly enjoyed myself and at the end of the week I was paid. I thought I was just doing it to help out and would have been satisfied with that. I felt needed and my self confidence had returned. I was upset at the end of the week that it was all over and hoped that when Wendy had her next holiday they would ask me again.

Little did I know that the other two practices which shared the health centre had been aware that I was covering Wendy and in no time at all I was covering Freda and Ann, too. One memorable week, when I was covering Ann who was out for several weeks after a hysterectomy, Wendy went off with a bad back and Freda fell over actually in the health centre and broke her arm – so I was covering all three practices!

Steve asked me to work a permanent five hours a week for his practice, arranging the cervical smear recalls, and I also learned how to do the switchboard, so I covered that when people were away too.

This really was a cure for depression! I slept like a log and awoke, keen and ready to go off to work again. Vic was quite able to manage the children, Emma was starting school and Nathan, nursery, so he ferried them about, did the washing and ironing and cooked the meals. He felt useful and so did I.

Whilst at work I became aware that the new physio- therapy department which was opening locally was adver- tising for a clerk/receptionist. I thought that would be just the job for me. Although I enjoyed working at the health centre, my contract was only for five hours a week and some weeks that was all I did work, another week it might be 35 hours! I did not know from one minute to the next and I usually had extra hours when the children were on holiday as staff at the health centre were off. The job in the physio- therapy department would be about 18 hours a week. I applied confident I would get an interview, and the next thing I heard was that someone had the job – I had not even had an interview. I could not understand it!

However, I still had my job at the health centre so I was no worse off. Then a few months later, the physiotherapy job was advertised again, so I applied again, and again I did not even get an interview.

However, the job at the health centre meant that we had some money again, and we bought a small caravan. With two friends we decided to go to the South of France, to the Camargue. Vic had never driven abroad, so in his typical fashion he decided to tow a caravan several thousand miles!

It was quite a journey. Our friends, Peter and Claire, had a Robin Reliant and a tent. We stopped every three hundred miles or so for the night all the way down to the South and thoroughly enjoyed witnessing the changing scenery and architecture. Once we got to St. Gilles we stayed put for a week and saw all we could. We went on a boat on Lake Vacares and saw flamingo, wild boar and the beautiful Camargue ponies.

We went to a "bull fight" in Arles, but in this contest the bull was the hero. The bull had rosettes on his horns and he went into the arena with 30 or so men, or razaters as they are known. Their aim is to remove the rosettes from the bull's horns without being injured themselves. After a certain length of time the bull is judged to have won if his rosettes are still intact. The older bulls know exactly what they are doing and tease the men. One bull was so proud when he won that he would not leave the arena until he had done several laps of honour. The younger bulls are not so clever or wily, but I am sure they soon learn. The bulls are never injured, and when they retire they can even have statues put up in their honour.

The razaters have fan clubs and at the time the favourite was Christian Chomel. Outside the arena there were stalls selling posters and booklets about him. Claire bought one such booklet for us all to read later. When we got in the arena the police were very helpful and found us excellent seats, helping Vic up the steps. It was very hot sitting in the old Roman arena, but we enjoyed ourselves immensely. Then we saw Christian Chomel standing just below us. Frantically we tried to find a paper and pen to ask for his autograph, but the moment had gone and we missed him. Later we read the booklet and found that he insisted that no one should speak to him on the day of a contest until after the event and he needed to be silent and alone! Everyone in the arena knew that, except us, and we almost committed an enormous *faux pas*!!

As we left the arena we literally bumped into him and we got him to autograph the booklet and had a brief word with him.

We really enjoyed our holiday and Vic was particularly thrilled to go into a church in *Sainte-Marie-de-la-Mer*, to see a statue of St Sarah, patron saint of gypsies and travellers. He bought a poster of her which hangs on our dining wall to this day.

When I got back to work, I was asked to go and work at the physiotherapy department to cover the clerk who was on holiday. I felt like saying something rather rude – but I talked it over with the family and decided I would do it. How glad I was that I did not get the job. I was so bored! It was alright for two weeks, but that was about as much as I could take. However, it bought us a dishwasher.

Chapter Eight

My cousin Terry had married my friend Sue and they had both pursued their careers and not had a family. She had had a lot of gynaecological problems and it seemed unlikely that she would conceive. However, just after Denise died she found that she was pregnant with Richard who was born four months after Nathan, and two years later, with Timothy. My Auntie Marjorie was widowed just a few weeks after Richard's birth and Terry and Sue bought a big house and built an extension for Auntie Marjorie to live in.

Terry was always working on the house, and in many ways we did not see a lot of him, but when there was a problem he was there. He was a great help to my parents when Terry and Denise died and they thought a great deal of him.

One day when he was working on the house he pulled a muscle in his neck and whilst rubbing it found a lump on his head. He went to the doctor and in no time at all was in hospital having a biopsy. It turned out to be a malignant melanoma and he had to have a wide excision with skin grafts. There was no radiotherapy or chemotherapy which could have helped him, so they had to hope that the excision had done the trick. It was a devastating blow as the survival rate was not high. However, Sue and Terry tried to take the attitude that they should enjoy life while they could as none of us know what is round the corner.

Two years later Sue had her gall bladder removed and was disappointed to find that she still felt nauseous and bloated several weeks after the operation. She was sent for a scan as it was feared that she might have some malignancy. When she had her scan there was great hilarity. Her bloated feeling was because she was 16 weeks pregnant with twins! There was great excitement. Terry had recently started his own company and they had been altering the house for Sue to run a bed and breakfast business – but that had to go on hold.

Cousin Terry was present at the birth – first Andrew and then Sarah. We were all delighted. Terry was going for regular check-ups and all was well.

Chapter Nine

Peter and Claire, the friends with whom we went to the South of France, had several dogs, of which Poppy, a Jack Russell Terrier, was expecting puppies. They asked if they could give a puppy to Emma and Nathan for Christmas. We thought that would be a good idea – we had a large garden and the children loved dogs. Unfortunately as the pregnancy progressed, Poppy became very ill and had to have a hysterectomy, losing the puppies.

Peter and Claire were very upset and felt they had disappointed the children. We tried to reassure them and said that we would look around for a puppy ourselves. However, one day Peter phoned and said he had been to the Bristol Dogs' Home and there was a 12-week-old Jack Russell bitch; should he try to get her for the children? We said yes.

On the day she was able to be released from the dogs' home, Peter was queuing up before 8.00 a.m. to make sure of getting her. He took her back to his work for the morning, where she stank the place out! Peter took her home at lunch time to Claire who gave her a bath – when lots of her fur dropped out to reveal flea bites all over her! So it was a small, half-bald but sweet smelling puppy who arrived at our house that evening.

She was immediately given the name of Daisy and we all fell in love with her. She had such an appealing face. She cried the first night and I went down to her and bathed all her inflamed bites, she was so grateful. After a few days she developed kennel cough and it was obvious that she had round worms, but she also had tape worms. She was a poor specimen! We took her to the vet and got all the right treatment for her. I was working at the Health Centre, so I was able to bring home slightly out of date babies' food or milk for her, and soon built her up. In fact when I was out with her about a month later, someone said to me, "I see you had to get rid of that other dog then, this one looks a lot more healthy." They did not believe she was the same dog.

She had a lovely temperament and allowed the children to play with her. She spent a lot of time with Vic and seemed to realise that he was not very agile. He was also having trouble with his hearing and she would tell him when the phone was ringing or someone was at the door. However, she could be naughty. Sometimes when Vic went up to the back lawn she would take one of his sticks from under him and make him fall over, then she would take it just out of his reach and bark at him! Yet she never did this when he was on concrete. It is obvious when she is laughing and she used to find it very funny when Vic fell over. She often would jump on his back and jump up and down having a lovely time. Of course, he used to laugh too, so it was quite a while before he could get back on his feet.

Sue welcomes you into her specially
designed kitchen

Sue enjoys a camel ride on a recent holiday in Israel

FUN

TIMES

Emma with
a python

(Above) Emma, Nathan   (right) Sue, dressed up as
                                            Burglar Betty for
                                            Bookday at school.

(Below) Victor looking after a pony: His professional
experiences in the circus made him keen for the children to
learn to ride.

THE DAILY BATTLE WITH TECHNOLOGY

Things are rarely designed with small people in mind! Some examples of the make-arounds that fill the life of Sue's family.

More adapting to things:
a special, low sink (right),
and Sue with Head teacher
at the school Christmas
Bazaar — Dick
Whittington and his cat!

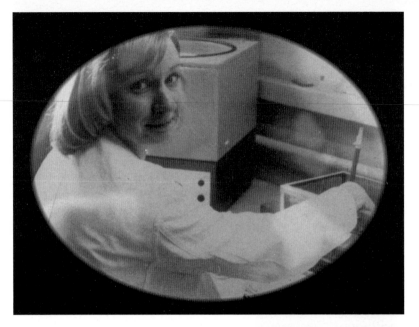

(Clockwise from top) Sue's sister
Denise, a laboratory technician.

Terry & Denise

Sue's parents,
Grandad with
Nathan; Nannie
with Emma.

All the family:

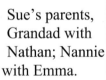 

Clockwise from top:
•The great day: November 10th 1973
•A family picnic, including Daisy.
•Emma steals a mince pie!
•Sue with her best friend Jenny, the smallest with the tallest in the class.

Victor's career in the Circus (before he met Sue). A 'genuine' performance of Snow White, plus some mementos. Circus does provide employment and opportunity to learn about the world while catching the public's eye.

Chapter Nine

It seemed that we would never get Daisy house-trained! There used to be puddles every morning, and sometimes during the day too. I felt the whole house smelled of it. One day I had had enough and I marched into the room saying "That is it. Either that dog goes or I do". There was silence and then Nathan (aged 3) looked up and said quite seriously, "But you will come and visit us won't you Mum?" I thought I had better keep quiet.

Eventually, Daisy did become house trained and now she only wets indoors if she wants to teach us a lesson. If we go on holiday and leave her in kennels, she will wet on our beds when we get back. Or if one of the children goes away for a few days they have to make sure their doors are shut or they might well come back to a wet bed. Daisy is now 15 and has almost stopped this.

Daisy has been such a lovely pet. She is so loving and faithful. She has been marvellous company for Vic. To Emma she is a real friend, and the confidante of many of her secret thoughts.

Chapter Ten

A change of direction. About this time Emma's local village school announced that it would be closing the next year. Nathan was due to start in the September and we decided that we would change Emma so that she and Nathan could go together. Emma would have one more year in the Infants and Nathan would have three years. We looked ahead to when they would need secondary schooling and discovered that one local school, although not the nearest, actually had a unit to cater for the needs of disabled children. This made us think that we would send our children to a feeder school for that secondary school and this is what we did – sending them to Broadway Infants School, just around the corner from my parents' home.

I carried on at the health centre, still with rather erratic hours, but Vic was always available to collect the children from school if I was working.

At the end of her infant years Emma went to the Junior school next door and Nathan went into his second year.

Chapter Ten

When I was in school one day, the acting Head asked me if there was an organisation which we belonged to as it was their custom to give their harvest collection to a charity and she felt that a charity with an association with one of the pupils was appropriate. I said that ARRG would be very happy to accept this, and arranged for someone to come and collect the cheque. The very day that we went in, the acting Head was in a turmoil. The school secretary had given in her notice as she had got a job nearer to her home. I said "That is a nice job for someone" – she turned to me and said "Would you like it?" She then looked into it and found she had to advertise it internally, but she still needed someone to do it on a temporary basis, so I agreed. I still kept on my five hours at the Health Centre, but spent 20 hours a week in school.

At first balancing the dinner money at the end of the week defeated me. I would take hours and it began to get me down, but I prayed about it and it began to fall into place. Although the post was advertised internally, there were no suitable applicants. After a while it was advertised externally and I was able to apply. I was interviewed with one other person, and the choice fell on me. Overjoyed, I could see the hand of God in this appointment; I had desperately wanted the physiotherapy job, but God had something so much better in store for me. A job where I was at home in the holidays with my children – and all because I was in the right place at the right time. God is so good. He also likes a laugh.

When I first got married I was so worried about having children – only because I did not want to take them to an infant school as I was sure all the children would stare at me and make fun of me. I tried to work out ways whereby my children could get to school and I need never appear on the scene, but that obviously was not practical and I ended up rather apprehensively at first, taking them to nursery and then infant and junior schools. I am sure God smiled to himself about the irony of me actually working in an infant school.

I gave in my notice at the Health Centre and had some lovely gifts and letters of thanks from the doctors I had worked for and in many ways I was very sorry to leave, but I wanted to have "my" job, with "my "desk, not just to use someone else's when they were away.

At first Nathan used to hide under my desk and refuse to go to his class, often "escaping" during the day and refusing to leave me, but he settled down and got used to me being in the school. He was quite naughty and was always being sent to the Head, which was quite embarrassing. He also used to threaten other children and when parents came to make an appointment to see the Head and looked very embarrassed I used to guess that they wanted to complain about Nathan – I was often right! On his first day in the school he had flooded the toilets by squirting the water from the water fountain all over the floor. He also spilled powder paint on the carpet by rushing round the classroom one day and knocking it off the table. He and his friend decided to clean it up, so they got some water... The carpet was never the same again, and he and his friends had to bring in some of their pocket money to pay for a carpet cleaner. They also had to write to the caretaker to apologise. Nathan's letter started – Dear Mrs. Brain, I am sore (sorry)!

When we went to parents evenings the teacher always started "What can I say, Emma works so hard, always listens, always tries to be helpful, she is a real pleasure to have in the class" Nathan's teachers always started "What can I say, Nathan does not work, never listens, distracts the class..."

I really enjoyed the job. I worked Monday, Wednesday and Fridays so I had Thursdays free and I always spent this with my Mum. Vic had started to attend the local Day Centre every Thursday. He was picked up by bus so I had the car and Mum and I used to go shopping, or just out for a ride. I always used to set her hair and then pick up the children and we had tea with her and Dad before going home.

Gradually the work load increased and I started to work several hours on a Tuesday morning, and then an hour on a Thursday, but still I kept the rest of the day free for Mum. Vic's pain increased yet again and his consultant recommended another operation. This time they wanted to operate in two places, one in his neck and one at the bottom of his spine. We were really worried that the operation on his neck could affect the use of his arms, especially as he relied so much on his arms to help him get around. But once again after a great deal of prayer we took the medical advice and Vic went ahead with the surgery. Mum had had one hip replacement in the winter and Vic's previous operation had been in January. It always seemed that we were battling our way through the snow to visit them and this time was no exception. This time when Vic went home, he had the full use of his arms, but he had lost a bit more of his mobility and although the pain was slightly less, it had certainly not gone.

We were disappointed. It seemed that Vic had gone through so much but he was no better.

Around about this time I was asked to be a deacon in the church. This was a great honour and I felt humble and proud at the same time to serve my Lord in this way. I thoroughly enjoyed my four years as a deacon. I tend to feel I am imposing if I call on or phone someone I do not know very well, but having a pastoral list of about 30 people, I soon got over this feeling and very much enjoyed getting to know folk with whom I had had little contact. It was a great privilege to lead the congregation in prayer before the communion service. I always prayed about this and wrote down what I wanted to say and on every occasion, except one, my prayer fitted in with the theme of the service. On this one occasion, it really seemed to have no relevance to the service which had gone on before, and I was beginning to panic. However, nothing else came to mind and I prayed the prayer I had prepared. After the service a lady came to me in tears and thanked me for the prayer which she said had helped her with something which had been a real burden to her. God was working his purpose out yet again!

Chapter Eleven

Alan and his wife Shirley and Vic and I saw each other regularly. Shirley and I discovered that we both had a desire to go to the Holy Land. We had a different minister at our church then, John Quinn, and he regularly took people on tours of the Holy Land and he, of course, encouraged us to go. He brought some slides round one evening and Shirley and I became very enthusiastic. It was a lot of money, but we decided that we would go.

I had always had a fear of flying and I was trying to overcome that. Everything was arranged at home – Vic would look after the children, Alan would come out some days and they would take the children out for the day. Meals were organised, Mum and Dad would help out and at last the great day dawned. I went in to get the children up as they were to go with Vic to take me in to catch the coach from Bristol to Heathrow Airport. Then Emma started – "I don't want you to go Mummy. What if the plane crashes?" She was echoing my thoughts exactly at that moment, but I did not want her to know that. All of a sudden I looked out of the window and there, in a clear sky, was a rainbow and I just knew it was God's promise to me that I would return safely and I told the children. They were quite content as we all felt that God had spoken to us.

When we got to Heathrow, I was rather overawed by the whole procedure, never having flown before. We flew on El Al, the Israeli airline, who are notoriously safety-conscious, and we were particularly intimidated by their repeated questioning as to whether we had left our bags unattended. In our party was the lady minister of St George Baptist Church, Bristol, and she had to unpack all her luggage for a search.

Around this time there had been several plane crashes all involving jumbo jets, so I was quite happy to go on any plane but a jumbo jet. Fortunately I could not see out of the window as we walked along the walkway to the plane, as our plane was a jumbo jet. By the time we reached the plane it was too late and I had to board with everyone else. I was shaking and I kept trying to remember God's promise to me. However, when we took off I was enthralled and so began a love of flying that has continued. We landed at Tel Aviv late at night and were taken to our hotel just on the edge of Jerusalem. The view in the morning was spectacular – the golden dome dominating the scene. I could not wait to start our tour and the first day we went along the *Via Dolorosa* – the way of the cross. When we got to the Holy Sepulchre I was so disappointed. It was so ornate and it seemed to me as if the various churches which laid claim to a small area inside the building were all trying to outdo each other in their decoration. This did not seem to be of Christ to me. We could file into a tiny room where it was said Jesus's body had lain, and inside was a priest who wanted money in order to let us hold a candle. I am afraid I refused. I had a vision of Jesus in the temple turning over the tables of the money changers; I also felt claustrophobic and wanted to get out into the fresh air. Was this what Isreal was like?

Another day we went along the Mount of Olives. This was more as I imagined the Holy Land to be. I could imagine Jesus in his white robes walking here. I was particularly impressed by the church Dominus Flavus - the master wept. It was here that Jesus stopped to weep over Jerusalem and I could have wept too. A few days before we had got there a tourist had been shot, the Arabs and the Jews were not happy together, the Moslems had charge of the temple, and all in all it was such a troubled city – yet so beautiful. To me it seemed symbolic of the way our Lord must weep over our world with all the trouble we have caused in it.

We also went to Bethany – the place our house is named after. We looked inside the tiny houses where so many live – a seeming impossibility.

On our last day in Jerusalem we went to the Garden Tomb – or Gordon's Calvary as it is also called. Here I felt at peace. In this simple garden, amongst a profusion of beautiful flowers and plants, we had communion and remembered what our Lord had done for us. This was a memory which where ever I am, or what ever I am doing, can still renew that peace within me.

Just outside our hotel was a minaret and every morning at sunrise the faithful would be called to prayer. Of course it woke us very early each morning and it was then difficult to get back to sleep again. I consoled myself with the thought of the devout man who every morning climbed the tower to conduct this ritual. I felt extremely cheated when I was told that the call was produced by a tape recorder on a time switch!

We left Jerusalem and went to Tiberias on the Sea of Galilee. Here wherever I looked I could see Jesus striding over the fields, his white robes flowing, surrounded by children and adults thirsting to hear him speak. We went to the Mount of the Beatitudes, Capernaum, and all the little towns around the lake where Jesus walked with his disciples.

One day we went to Masada – the hill fortress where the Jews held out against the Romans until, on the eve of capture, they all committed suicide. We had to go up in a cable car and then walk the rest of the way. I was very proud to have managed it and bought the T-shirt to prove it! On the very top, with temperatures well over 100 F. gerbils ran around our feet as we walked.

We bathed in the Dead Sea – I did not float like everyone else – instead I was thrown violently on one side with my mouth under water! My eyes stung and I was more than pleased to get out and stand under the showers on the beach to cool them down. Not an experience to be repeated – but definitely one which has to be done once in a life time.

One day we went to Acre – where a town has been discovered under the town. It was fascinating and we all queued up to go inside to look. We did not realise that we were not supposed to just walk around, but we had to stand in each room whilst a party of Arabs put on a play in arabic. When their sketch was over they would lead the way into the next area. After about two of these we began to get bored - we could not understand a word and the sketches seemed mostly to consist of a great deal of sword waving and not much else. We had a hurried discussion and decided to walk ahead of the players at a convenient moment when we could without interrupting their play. We were to meet the coach in a while and wanted to see more of the town above. Very quietly we moved around the players and started to go on. However, they did not like it at all and gave chase brandishing their swords. At one point they slammed a door on the leg of someone in our party and caused some damage to a ligament. I was terrified. I had taken my wheelchair on the holiday and all the members of the party were really good about pushing me and I never felt a nuisance. We ran on ahead of these arabs and they were putting the lights off as we went. We came to some stairs and I got out and went down the steps and kept on running. John Quinn was running behind me with the wheelchair shouting, "Sue, Sue, get in" and apparently I said (I was too terrified to remember!) "I'm not coming back – I'll get in when you catch up with me." and I just kept on running, faster than anyone had ever seen me run before!! Everyone was laughing – but they kept running too and eventually we reached daylight and got out. John always said that he would use that in one of his sermons. I wonder if he ever did.

John was so good in encouraging me to do everything on the trip. He would lie dreadfully and say "Come on, Sue, it is just down those few steps and around the corner" so I would go only to find it was just down the steps, round the corner, down more steps, round more corners and down more steps! However, John would catch hold of one arm and someone else on the other side and I managed to do everything.

At last the time came to return home. One day I hope to return to the Holy Land. Inspite of the turmoil which exists in that beautiful place, it is where God chose to send his Son and is a very special place.

We all enjoyed holidays in the caravan. Everything in our caravan was at a low level, it had been made like that, so we managed well. We went on a church camping weekend to a place called Fiddington, near Bridgwater and had a lovely time. The owners were helpful and friendly and that encouraged us to think we could go off on our own. We spent many happy days at Fiddington, where Mike and his boys were always willing to help with the awning or anything else we could not manage. The camp had plenty to do for the children and we really enjoyed ourselves.

One day we were all packed up and ready to be off down to Fiddington - I had phoned Mum and said goodbye and was just looking round the house to make sure windows were shut, etc. when the phone rang. I few months earlier Vic had seen a cutting in a newspaper saying "Are you under 4'? Would you like to earn 70 pounds a day? If so write to this address" It was for a film and promised that all small people would be treated with respect. I had said to Vic that as there was four of us we should reply and we had done so. We had completely forgotten all about this and when I picked up the phone and a voice said "Mrs. Phillips?" I thought it was going to be a double glazing salesman. Instead it was the film company asking us to go to London immediately for a fitting. As this was half term it was alright, but the filming would be the following week when I should have been at work. I phoned my Head and she agreed to me having time off – I had worked extra days and was owed time off anyway – so I phoned the film company and agreed to go. I picked up the phone again and said to Mum "Change of plan – we're off to London to have a costume fitting to appear in a film". She was flabbergasted as we had not even told her about the advert, it seemed of such little importance.

Off we went to London, Elstree studios, had our fittings and went back down to Fiddington for a few days, prior to going back up for the film, Willow. We arranged to take our caravan and leave it in Vic's cousin's garden which was fairly near where the film was to be shot in the grounds of Brockett Hall.

We had to be on the set at 6.30 a.m. each day and did not leave until about 8.00 p.m. each evening. We were given enormous meals all day long and looked after well. The weather was wet and miserable, but that did not matter. My feet are quite fat and I often have to have shoes a bit too long to get them wide enough. I had to have wellington boots for the film – they were much too large and the wardrobe department cut them down so that they were below my knee. As I walked along they made a very rude noise. I got redder and redder as the camera crew made such comments as "It must have been the scrambled egg for breakfast, or the baked beans" until finally, when everyone was in hysterics, the wardrobe man cut holes in the toes so that they did not make a noise. The holes let in the mud, but that was preferable to the rude noises!

After the first day the children were so tired they wanted to go home, but we encouraged them to keep going and they ended up thoroughly enjoying themselves. We used to get back to the caravan each evening and I would wash the children and put them to bed. The next day I would wash them again and we would get to the location where we had mud smeared all over us – Emma and Nathan could not see why I made them wash all the week! Lots of our small friends from the Association were also in the film so in between takes we had a good old gossip and lots of fun.

The director of the film was Ron Howard (Richie Cunningham of Happy Days fame). In one take he wanted two boys to play a game with sticks and Nathan and another boy (a Spaniard) were chosen. They started to play and the Spanish boy who would have made two of Nathan really entered into the role and I thought he would kill Nathan! Nathan suddenly threw down his stick and marched up to Ron Howard and said "I'm not doing that any more unless you tell him he hasn't got to hurt me." After some discussion an interpreter was found who did explain to the Spanish boy that it was a game.

We filmed for four days and although we did not see any of the big stars of the film like Val Kilmer and Joanne Whalley, it was an experience of a life time. Vic never actually appeared in the film – or if he did we have yet to spot him. But he met up with an old friend from his circus days and spent a lot of the time splicing ropes for the ponies on the set. However he still got paid. We were all just extras, very much blink and you miss us, but it was great fun and we would not have missed it for the world. It was quite an anticlimax when we had to come back down to earth and return home to work.

One Sunday we went to church and then went straight down to Fiddington. As we got there the children were hungry, but we could not do much about getting any food ready until the awning was up. The chap in the next caravan offered to give us a hand, as Mike was busy for a few minutes. We got talking and said that we had been late in arriving as we had been to church. He turned out to be a vicar and he and his wife became great friends with us. A few caravans along there was a man who wore a badge saying "Smile Jesus Loves You", so we made ourselves known to him as well. In the evenings Boots and Den, the occupants of the other caravan, and Vic and I would play Trivial Pursuit and sing songs from Mission Praise.

We kept in touch with Boots and Den and met them a few times at Fiddington. One year they came full of enthusiasm for the church holiday they had just been on and asked us to go with them the following year. The holiday was at a Christian centre called Gaines. We were doubtful as we would know no-one except Boots and Den and their children, but carried along by their enthusiasm we agreed.

In the summer of 1988 we went off to Gaines. What an experience! We had no knowledge of the charismatic movement and here were people talking and singing in tongues, and dancing in the spirit. It was wonderful. The 110 people there were all strangers when we arrived, but friends by the evening. The songs were lively and people clapped and held their hands in the air. There was Bible teaching in the morning and evening and the rest of the day we were free to do as we pleased. Emma and Nathan made friends and we hardly saw them the whole holiday.

There was an indoor pool there. I had taken my swimming costume but I don't know why as I could not swim and hated the water. I used to take the children swimming at our

local disabled club and they were both competent swimmers, but although I had had lessons for years as a child, I
still could not swim and "people who knew about such
things" said that my centre of gravity was wrong and I never
would swim.

One young man there, Roy, asked me why I wasn't
swimming when the children were such good swimmers. I
had to admit that I could not swim and he offered to teach
me. I explained that my centre of gravity was not compatible
with swimming, but he said that was rubbish, and he would
teach me. Finally, to prove him wrong, I agreed to go to the
pool with him. He was very persistent and insisted on me
trying over and over again and then finally said we had to
return the next day when he was sure I would be better. He
really did not have much patience with me having a panic
every time my face got wet – I was swimming on my back,
and I felt goaded to try again.

One of the other people on the holiday, Mandy, was such
a spiritual person I asked her to pray for me while I was in
the water as I got in such a panic when my face got wet. She
said she would come down to the pool and then I would
actually see her praying so I would stay calm. We splashed
about in the shallow end for a while and then Roy said
"Come on, you can try a length". In great fear and trepida-
tion, I started off, frightened to breathe, but I felt hands
around my waist holding me up and so I relaxed and swam
to the far end of the pool. When we got there Roy was
beaming and said "I told you you could swim". I smiled at
him and said "Yes, but it would have been different if you
weren't holding me." "I wasn't holding you" Roy said, and
Mandy backed him up. Suddenly I knew whose hands had

Chapter Eleven

been holding me up, but I was to learn the significance of this later on.

There was great rejoicing on the holiday over my swim and while singing the chorus"I'm walking in faith and victory, for the Lord my God is with me" we substituted "I'm swimming in faith and victory!"

We really enjoyed that holiday and all too soon it was over and we returned home, singing the new songs we had learned, such as Shine Jesus Shine and keen for them to be included in our church programme.

Chapter Twelve

Denise's birthday had been on 19th August and we always made it a practice to pop in to see Mum on that day. 1988 was no exception. For some time Dad had been having some funny turns. He went blank for a while. He had had to forfeit his driving licence for a year after one episode, but generally he was better. On this occasion he had had another slight turn, but the weather had been very hot and Mum had put it down to this. Nevertheless, she was worried. We had a cup of tea and a biscuit and I noticed that Mum had trouble in swallowing her biscuit. I went cold. I had been a medical secretary for long enough to know what that probably meant and I knew we were going to lose her. I asked her how long she had been having trouble and she said just that day and she put it down to worry about Dad, but I went out and used her phone to make an appointment for her to see Steve, our G.P.

When she went to see Steve he asked her what was wrong and she said "Nothing, it is just Sue fussing!" Apparently,

Steve said that he was going to fuss too and sent her for an X-ray. I took her for the X-ray just as Emma started at her secondary school. She then went back for an oesophagoscopy. She was under Dr. Harvey and he was very kind to her and she had confidence in him. After the oseophagoscopy she came home for the weekend and was so ill, I could see her fading in front of me. I phoned Steve on the following Monday and said to him "My Mum is dying in front of me" and he said to me, "You know what is wrong with her, I really don't think there is any hope". He phoned the hospital and talked to Dr. Harvey who arranged for her to be admitted for more tests. As by this time Mum could hardly swallow anything, they asked the general surgeons to see her with a view to some palliative surgery. Mr. May was the surgeon who came to see her. He agreed to operate and the operation was scheduled for 13th October, Denise and Terry's wedding anniversary.

I could not understand why this was happening and I remember being so angry with God. "Why are you taking the children's granny" I shouted to Him. "You have taken their auntie and any hope of cousins, why their granny?" But God understands our anger and eventually he gave me peace. It was then that I realised the significance of the arms I had felt holding me up when I learned to swim. God wanted to show me that he was supporting me.

At about three o'clock the phone went at work. It was Mr. May. "I'm so sorry Sue, " he said "There was nothing I could do, the cancer went the whole length of her intestine." I felt so sorry for him. We had had a good relationship when I was his secretary and it had fallen to him to operate on my sister and now my mother, and in both cases he had been unable to save their lives. It was then my job to go around to tell my father. He had never believed that she would die before him and he was lost. He sent me home to get the children's tea and I arranged to go with him into the hospital later that night. When I got home I phoned our Minister, Tony, and he went straight down to sit with him for a while. Mum came around from the anaesthetic and I think she could tell by the lack of tubes etc. that not much surgery had been carried out. All she wanted to do was to go home and Steve was wonderful in the way he arranged for this, providing a district nurse and putting us in touch with our local hospice.

After about a week, Mum came home. We brought her bed downstairs and spent every available minute with her. Her swallowing was getting worse and worse and her legs swelled, but she was still enjoying life and interested in all going on around her. Dad had always been a good cook and he would try all sorts of things to tempt her to eat – sometimes she could, but more and more often she could not. One day Auntie Marjorie came over and said Terry had been for his five year check following his melanoma and had been given the "all clear" and discharged. We were all so pleased.

Those three weeks are some of the most precious in my life. Mum and I talked freely about everything. Many people sent her cards, flowers and little booklets. Mum had always been very shy and retiring and it was good that she was able to see her popularity by the number of people who were in touch one way or another. We read the Bible daily together and I shared with her something I had read. When a baby is in its mother's womb it thinks 'this is perfect, I am kept warm, nourished – what could be better'? Then it is born, and it looks up into its mother's face, sees her smile and sees the love she has for it and thinks, 'no, this is perfection'. If God has brought us through this so far, surely the next step really is perfection and the God who was with us all though our birth will be with us all through our dying.

Mum chose the hymns she wanted at her funeral and mentioned items or possessions she wanted passed on to various people. There was no pretence, but no sadness. Each day was very special.

Emma and Nathan visited regularly and brought their friends in. On the 12th November, Emma and her friend Helen went shopping and bought Mum a carnation all wrapped up beautifully. They brought it in to her and then sat on the floor as she was on the bed and played a game of cards. It was all so relaxed and natural. That day Mum asked me to get some wool for her to knit some bedsocks. The next day she got quite sleepy and in the afternoon she said to me "I am going to be with Jesus soon" I asked her if she was frightened and she replied "No, I have never been less frightened about anything in my life. I shall see Denise and my mum and dad. You will come after me." She had moments that afternoon when I am sure she could see what was ahead of her. As there had been ever since the beginning of her illness, there was an aura of peace around her, one which gave strength to all those who visited her. On the Monday morning, Vic and I, Emma and Nathan went in before school and spoke to her – she wished us all a good day. Her friend Lorna called in and her sister Marjorie came over early – it seemed as if she had said good bye to those most dear to her and after 9.30 a.m. she did not speak again. I briefly went into school to do the dinner money, but left about 10.00 a.m. and spent the rest of the day sitting by her and holding her hand. She died at 4.00 p.m. If I was not a Christian before I am sure I would have been then. I could see her soul leaving her body which became an empty shell. I hardly recognised it as my mother, because all that she was had gone and all that life force had to go somewhere – where else but with her Lord?

I phoned Tony, our minister, to tell him that Mum had gone and he came down that night to Dad's house, as did Cousin Terry and Sue. Terry had not been very well that day with a sickness bug, but he helped Tony take Mum's bed back upstairs and we had a good evening. Tony made us laugh as he said that Arthur Liston (the minister who had married us) had once been the minister of his home church and that he had always meant to tell Mum that as he knew she held him in high regard, but he had always forgotten. He said that he could imagine Arthur and Mum in heaven at that very moment, with Arthur saying to Mum "Well, what is wrong with that Tony Marron that he never told you that!"

I felt that the funeral was truly a celebration of Mum's life. There were lots of people in the church and I felt happy that she was as she had said, with Denise and her mum and dad. I had tried to get a black coat for the funeral, but I could not so I wore my old one and a friend said to me "Did you get a new coat?" I said "You were there, surely you saw I had my old one on". To which my friend replied "I was just looking at your face as you looked so happy". The Christians at least in the congregation understood my feelings and I hope I did not upset anyone by the look on my face.

Terry was still not well at the funeral. He was still vomiting and had been to the doctor who felt that it was due to shock over my mother's death. He looked pale but he was interested to meet my other cousin Terry from Cornwall who had also recently started his own business and they arranged to get together with a contract in mind which would benefit both firms.

By the next week, Terry was no better and his GP sent him into hospital for tests. Two weeks to the day of mum's funeral he was told that he was dying. His malignant melanoma had spread to his stomach, liver and spleen and there was no treatment which would help him. He was 42 year old, the boys were 9 and 7 and the twins were just three years old.

In the same way that Mum had faced death with quiet dignity, so did Terry. I told Tony, our minister, and he went over several times to be with Terry, having met him at Dad's house on the day Mum died, he felt he knew him enough to visit. Terry enjoyed his visits, but whether they were on a spiritual level or not, I do not know.

Terry wanted to have Christmas at home with his family and this he did, going to bed on Boxing Day and dying on January 3rd. I saw him minutes before he died when I said "I'll see you Terry" To which he smiled and replied faintly "Yes".

Our family seemed to have its tragedies in pairs – with six weeks or so in between. It was very hard to cope with this. Dad in particular was devastated and became very depressed. He had looked on Terry as a son and he felt so sorry for his four children. I was so pleased when Sue asked our minister Tony to speak at Terry's funeral. The church was absolutely packed, with lots of people standing outside. Tony spoke of the quality of Terry's life as evidenced by the vast number of people who were at the funeral and said that many people may have a longer quantity, but it was the quality which counted. For a long time afterwards I worried about whether Terry had been a Christian. As a child he had gone to church but this had stopped during his teens. I felt that when faced with his own mortality he must have made a decision one way or another but I did not know and I worried and worried. One day following my usual Bible reading a verse leapt off the page at me "I know a good man and I will judge him, said the Lord". I was at peace. This was a message for me and I could let the matter drop. It was marvellous, I felt such a relief. A few days later someone from church phoned me and shared a similar worry that she had about a relation. I told her how I had been helped by this particular verse and that I could find the reference for her as I remembered which day I had read it – it was just a few verses after my reading for the day. I looked and looked, but it was not there. Perhaps it was another day and I looked up the readings for days around that date, all to no avail. God had sent that verse for me.

Chapter Thirteen

I always think that one of the nicest things about getting older is that I can look back and see how God has had his hand on my life, which gives me great confidence for the future. I often think of the hymn "All I have needed Thy hand hath provided" I might want a lot – but I always have what I need. Over the years we had often been helped in the garden by boys who were having to do community service for some misdemeanour or another. Some boys were quite good, others hopeless, but in the main they were all nice lads and we were glad to have them in our home. They were often taken aback when we said grace before the Sunday meal, but after a while they got the hang of it and would often say "Grace, Nathan" if he picked up his fork before it had been said. We had some very in-depth conversations with some of them and I do pray that seeds were sown.

All of a sudden this source of help seemed to dry up. I felt that we should not have drug users at our house, bearing in mind that we had two young children, and all the offend-

ers seemed to have convictions for drug abuse. Then someone told me about our local open prison and I approached
them for help. They sent us Trevor and said that he could
come each Saturday and Sunday. We had to go to the prison
and pick him up and return him in the evenings. He was a
lifer who had been in prison for over twenty years. Ours was
the first private house he had been in for all that time. He
did not have much idea about gardening, but he was keen to
learn and was so helpful. His first day with us was his
birthday, so I made him a cake and he was delighted. He
loved to come to church with us on Sundays and made
friends with many of the congregation. He was invited to
accompany us to a dedication meal after the service in
church and he has never forgotten that. We got on really well
with Trevor and became very fond of him. We did not know
what his crime was, we just felt that was his business.

As winter came on there was not much that Tevor could
do – and he hated being shut inside the house. We mutually
agreed that it would be better if he could get a placement
somewhere where he could work outside, winter as well as
summer and we could have someone who could do some
decorating for us. Trevor very rarely had visitors and used
to invite us to events which were held at the prison, so we
saw him often and kept in touch. He had a home leave every
so often and he would spend these with his sister in the north
of England. He had one just after Christmas and was looking
forward to it.

I got home from work one day to find that Trevor had
been accused of an attempted rape on his way back from
home leave and had gone on the run. His original crime had
been rape. The police phoned us and asked us to report him

if he contacted us. We felt so sorry for him. It was a very cold, miserable night and I asked the police to let me know if and when they found him as I did not want to think of him being scared out there somewhere. Eventually the police phoned and said he had been found. I asked them to give him a message – sending our love.

I found out which prison he had been taken to and phoned the chaplain there asking how Trevor was. He was in very low spirits and I kept sending messages to him. He did not want to see anyone but eventually he sent us a visitors pass. It was a very tearful reunion on both sides. Trevor wanted to reassure us that in spite of his record he would never have hurt Emma or me, and I was able to truthfully say to him that I had never for one moment imagined that he would. The friends at church rallied round wonderfully and sent him messages and some even visited him. Trevor was astounded that he was shown so much love after what he had done. I hated to visit Trevor in Bristol Prison. I used to shake before I got there and that lasted for several hours. I did not realise how awful it must be for parents who have to visit sons in prison, to see them locked away and I was glad that the children came with us one day, so that they could see what prison was really like. He was in the company of some quite notorious criminals. It was so different from Leyhill Open Prison, where I felt quite at home.

After Trevor came to trial he was sent to a maximum security prison in the north, but we continue to write and he phones regularly. He is now very involved with the church group in his prison and has provided prayer support for us on numerous occasions. He has made a beautiful wall hanging for our church which says "Blessed is the man whose trust is in the Lord". I do pray that he will continue to trust the Lord.

At that time I felt the time had come for me to be released from my duties as a deacon. This was not because of any lessening in my faith, rather because I felt that God wanted me to be free to serve him in a different way, and indeed I was led into the Prison Fellowship Ministry at Leyhill. Vic and I really enjoyed the fellowship we received there at the fortnightly meetings. After Trevor we had several more prisoners, some of whom we are still in contact with. Unfortunately with Vic's disability worsening it has made it difficult for us to collect the men in the mornings so for the present at least, we do not have any prisoners with us. However, God has sent us help in the shape of a neighbour who loves gardening. God always provides.

Chapter Fourteen

We spent a lot of time in Cornwall with my cousin Rosemary and her family. It became like a second home to us and whilst we were there we attended St. Austell Baptist Church where we were always made very welcome. One particular Sunday as we were in church God's Holy Spirit was felt very powerfully and I heard a voice say very loudly "Don't limit me". I looked around but everyone was just sitting still and had obviously heard nothing so I knew that it was a message for me. I did not understand what God meant, but I felt that I should let God have more control in my life and really trust him more.

Dad continued to be depressed and at times was very unhappy and difficult, yet at other times he was fine. Vic continued to deteriorate physically and it was getting more and more precarious for him to use the stair lift as he was so unsteady at the top when he tried to get on or off of it. I was always very worried when I went to work and was always glad when he phoned me to say he was up and downstairs.

He seemed to spend more and more time in bed. He got relief from the spasm in his legs when he was in the bath, but one day while he was in the bath his legs went into spasm and threw him backwards and he was unable to get up. We heard some funny noises from the bathroom and I went in to find Vic under the water. I was unable to pull him up and called Nathan who jumped into the bath, with all his clothes on, and pulled Vic up. After that we made sure someone was always with him when he had a bath.

At the back of our house were some out-buildings – a coal-shed (which we had always used for our deep freeze) a toilet and wash basin and a workshop. The workshop was full of tools, and all manner of bits and pieces – Vic is a real hoarder! When we were sitting out on our patio one evening with Alan and Shirley I said "If I was rich, I would like to turn the out-buildings into a utility room, bathroom and bedroom, so that Vic does not have to go up the stairs." Alan said that it would not cost that much to do and suggested that I look into it. He knew of a builder who would not charge too much and he would help himself. He sent out the builder and Dad advised us to go ahead and promised to back us financially if we got into trouble. We were in the process of buying the house from the council, so it would add to the value of the property.

We asked a friend at church to draw us up some plans but then Vic got worse and was sent to see a neurologist at Frenchay Hospital. He organised some tests but warned that he feared Vic would have to have another operation. We had planned a holiday in Norfolk and Vic was keen to go, so the four of us set off. We stayed in a chalet adapted for the disabled, where we had stayed before. When we got there

Emma and Nathan went off to the swimming pool and came back saying they were sure they knew two of the boys in the pool from Hill House, the Covenanter camp which they went on each summer. We thought that would be too much of a coincidence, but they went back and checked and sure enough, it was Darren and Daniel.

We went out and about around the local area, went to see Vic's friend David who had been our best man, and his wife Sally, and were having a lovely time, when very early on the Wednesday morning Vic looked a dreadful colour and collapsed on the bathroom floor. We were horrified and did not know what to do. When you are our size you cannot reach phone boxes very easily! We managed to get through to the doctor and he came immediately. Vic was lying on the bathroom floor saying to me "Lift me back into the wheelchair. Don't let the doctor do it, he might hurt his back." I don't know what he thought it would do to mine!!

It turned out that Vic had a severe urinary infection. He developed diarrhoea and vomiting and was delirious. I was very frightened. David had just had a hernia operation and was not allowed to drive and Sally does not drive, so it was no good relying on them. However, Darren and Daniel's parents were on hand, and they are strong Christians, so I did not feel so alone. Even in the wilds of Norfolk, 200 miles away from home, God provided.

We decided to go back home on the Friday rather than the Saturday as I would have to drive and we did not want to be held up by traffic jams in the heat. Vic had such a high temperature I wanted him to be kept cool. Vic lay on the back seat with Emma while Nathan navigated in the front and we drove home. Vic knew very little about the journey

– luckily for him as he hates my driving! At one point we stopped and went into a Little Chef for a meal, but Vic did not know.

By the following Tuesday he seemed to be sleeping a lot and was a funny colour. Dr. Campbell, the neurologist phoned to say he had the results of the tests and he felt Vic should be admitted some time. I said that I had just phoned our GP as I was very worried about him, so Dr. Campbell told me to take Vic straight to hospital and he would sort it out with the GP. This I did and Vic was admitted for what turned out to be a three month stay. His spinal problems had affected the nerves in his bladder and he was not emptying it sufficiently, hence he was in effect being poisoned. Fortunately his kidneys had not been damaged. He was catheterised and slowly improved.

However, tests showed that his spine was collapsing and more nerves were being crushed. Yet another operation was necessary and this time it was planned that the neurosurgeons would start it and the orthopaedic surgeons take over and put metal rods up Vic's spine. This was to be a long operation and by far the most serious he had had. In fact the operation lasted seven hours and because Vic had lain on his stomach for so long his gut went into spasm and he had to have a tube up his nose. He was high on pain killing drugs and kept pulling the tube out saying in great wonderment "I've got a hose up my nose". It was unfortunate that he had been on one ward and then was returned to another after his operation, so they did not know him at all. One day they stopped the morphine and started to give him pethedine. He talked utter rubbish. There were birds flying around the ward, goldfish on the ceiling, one of the prisoners had a dog in prison and I was supposed to know all about it – when I did not know what he was talking about he got cross. I knew it was the medication and I felt I was distressing him and that he might well sleep if I went home so that is what I did. I phoned later in the evening to find out how he was and the nurse I spoke to said "He is alright. I thought you were in earlier." I said that yes I had been in earlier, but that he had been talking rubbish. "Oh," said the Nurse, quite seriously "Doesn't he usually?"

We were very worried and at the same time I was trying to get going with the extension. Roy, from the prison, and I cleared out Vic's shed as best we could. We went to the local amenity site almost every day with car loads of rubbish and I am sure we threw out things we should have saved, but we did not have room for it all. The plans were for a utility room, a bathroom with wash basin, bidet, toilet and shower bath, and a bedroom. We extended the shed by 8' to accommodate this and it meant moving the garden shed and a manhole. We started to dig the foundations before the plans were passed – naughty I know, but time was pressing. It became very obvious that Vic would never be able to go upstairs again and the extension was a necessity.

The weather was really kind to us and not one day was lost because of it. The builders worked happily and every-thing went smoothly – it just had to as I had enough to cope with Vic in hospital.

During this time it was Emma's 16th birthday. Because she had mobility allowance she was able to learn to drive at 16 and Dad had always promised her a car for her birthday. We saw a lovely little red Mini Automatic, which she and I fell in love with, and Dad bought it for her. We booked a driving lesson for her on her birthday, but she was quite a timid driver at first and did not take to it straight away. I had been down to see Vic during the afternoon and he had had a sickness bug that morning, but he was getting over it, he seemed slightly washed out but nothing to worry about. That evening I went to the Prison Fellowship Meeting at Leyhill Prison. Emma wanted me to drive her car and so I did. As I usually drove Vic's Montego Estate which was also red, I had lots of comments such as "Did you go through the car wash and make it shrink?"

We had a lovely evening at Leyhill and many of the men asked me to pass on messages to Vic. As I drove out of the prison the car seemed to turn towards the hospital and I thought I would just drive down to see Vic for five minutes before going home. When I went on to the ward I thought at first that Vic was asleep, but when I could not rouse him and he was red hot to the touch I began to worry. The staff were all closeted in the office doing change over for the night staff and would not be disturbed, but then his doctor came on to the ward. I called to him and asked him to look at Vic. He said he thought he was all right, although he had been ill earlier, but I made him come over. As soon as he looked closely at Vic he realised all was not well. He said he was in the middle of examining a patient on the next ward and he would be straight back.

As he left the night staff started to come around and the nurse said to Vic "Why aren't you talking to your wife Vic?" "Because he is too ill" I said and then they looked at him and found his temperature was sky high. Windows were thrown open, a fan was brought and another nurse was sent to bleep the doctor. I said I had already called the doctor and he would be back. Vic's pulse was double what it should be and he was unrousable. The doctor came back and examined him. They never did find what caused it, but thanks to the nursing care he received that night, he recovered quickly. I cannot help wondering whether the night staff would have just thought he was asleep and left him and if so, whether he would be with us now. But the One who looks after us knew I had to go down to the hospital that night and He sent me there at exactly the right time. As you can imagine, when I did not return home at the usual time Emma was convinced I had crashed her mini, but I did manage to phone her from the hospital and explain what had happened.

From then on Vic continued to improve, albeit slowly. However, he had completely lost the use of his legs and bladder. It was quite a problem transferring from the bed to his wheelchair, wheelchair to toilet, etc. Vice has, like all people with achondoroplasia, short arms, and it made it very difficult to lever himself around. Many different methods were tried, but in the end it was sheer strength of will which made Vic completely independent again.

He came home from hospital at the beginning of the October half term. The extension was not finished so we "camped out" in the dining room, with the portaloo from the caravan as we had no downstairs toilet. He was given a care assistant, Rita, whose job it was to help him to find ways of doing things for himself. At first she came nearly all day, got him up and came back and put him to bed. This was gradually scaled down until she was just coming to get him up.

We moved into the extension on Christmas Eve! All the other times Vic had come home from hospital I had felt very isolated as he was always slightly worse mobility-wise but we had no advice or help. This time it was different and we were supported by the home care team, the occupational therapist, and most of all the district nurses on our practice who came for nearly two years each morning to get him washed, dressed and in his wheelchair. He had a hoist fitted which takes him from the bath to the toilet to the bidet. He shoots along a rail in a sling – which is quite funny, but it does mean that he is completely independent and safe in the bath. Gradually, Vic got more and more able to do things for himself, until now he gets himself up, washed and dressed.

For the first time, Vic's pain had lessened. Although he was less mobile, in a way being in the wheelchair permanently was better as he had been falling all over the place and cutting his head quite badly. Of course there was quite a lot of adapting to do. There is a lot of difference between being able to stand, even if for just a few minutes, and not being able to take any weight at all on the legs. We were stuck for a while about how to get Vic's wheelchair in the car, but we heard about a car hoist which is attached to the roof of the car and at the touch of a button takes the car up on to the roof of the car. We asked the local Round Table and Lions Clubs if they would help us and they were pleased to do so. This has made so much difference to Vic. He is now completely independent and is able to go out or stay in as he pleases.

Chapter Fifteen

Dad's mood swings were getting quite worrying and I felt on edge as I was usually needed to calm down situations which seemed to arise over nothing, but he was my father and I felt I had to do the best I could for him. In May, 1993, I was at work and I turned round to do some photocopying. I felt a pinching pain in my left hip – this often happened and sometimes it went as soon as it came, sometimes it left a soreness for a few days or even weeks. My hips were in a pretty poor state but I had been told about 20 years previously that hip replacements would not help me, so I had just put up with the pain and just done less and less.

However, on this occasion the pain got worse and worse and I went across to the desk to sit down on a low stool – I got half way down and could not get any further! I was stuck. The Head was in her office with the Adviser, but luckily it was break time and staff came down for their coffee. They realised I was in trouble and called the doctor. I felt so silly and found the whole thing amusing, although painful. He came and called an ambulance. As you can imagine, the infants in the school were thrilled to have Mrs. Phillips going off in an ambulance! I had to have gas and air to even get on the stretcher as my hip was so painful. Emma said "Other mothers go off and have gas and air and come back with a baby – why didn't you?" They never did find out what had happened as when they X-rayed me they could not make head nor tail of my hip joint. They X-rayed the right one for comparison, and found that was even worse! I was given bed rest for five days and the pain calmed down, but I was referred to an expert on replacement hips to see if he could do anything for me and, fortunately, he said he could. My name was put down for surgery in the Autumn. Dad was getting more and more unreasonable and had been physically violent to Emma. He began to frighten me and some of his neighbours were complaining to me of his behaviour. I tried to get him to see a doctor but he said nothing was wrong and was very aggressive. I was forced to stay away from him as I was frightened that he would damage my already precarious hips. I just could not understand it.

I kept praying about him and mentally I wrote a list of what I wanted in a father – it was not what I had at that time and I felt I was probably being idealistic anyway.

I was kept informed about him by my Auntie Marjorie, and she told me that he had seen the doctor and eventually prostate problems had been diagnosed and he had to go into hospital. I got our minister, Tony, to go around with me and we talked with him eventually, although for a long time he would not come out of the kitchen. I felt that I could go and see him in hospital and this I did, only to be met by a totally different, much nicer person.

I asked the sister on the ward if he had been difficult and she said that would have been the prostate trouble. When the bladder does not empty properly, urea is stored and the brain gets totally unreasonable. She said some men were "flying from the ceiling" in there, but once his bladder had been emptied properly he was fine.

He was back to calling me "my lovey" and he was everything on my mental list and more.

Unfortunately, the prostate turned out to be malignant and so Dad had to have hormone injections into his stomach everymonth, which were not very pleasant, but they seemed to do the trick in keeping the cancer at bay.

Chapter Sixteen

That summer we went to Hothorpe Hall, a Christian conference centre, where the hosts were Jen and Tony Larcombe. Jen and I had started a correspondence some time before when I wrote to tell her how much her books had helped me. Jen is so down-to-earth – I thoroughly recommend her books to anyone. She is not frightened to say that she gets tired, or angry – I feel so many Christian writers set unrealistically high standards and I find it so disheartening when I realise that I cannot live up to them. I almost felt she had given me permission to say sometimes "No, I cannot do that, I am too tired". Previously I had tried to physically keep up with everyone else, going to meeting after meeting, and my family had suffered as well as my own health.

Hothorpe was marvellous. There was such a sense of relaxation. The speaker was Ken Clarke from Northern Ireland and it was lovely to meet him and his family. We made lots of new friends and learned new songs. One of them burned into my heart:-

Faithful One,
So unchanging,
Faithful One,
You're my rock of peace.
Faithful One,
So unchanging,
I call out to you again and again
I call out to you again and again.
You're my rock in times of trouble,
You hold me up when I am down.
All through the storm your love is the anchor;
My hope is in you alone

God is so faithful: I'm not, but He is. As the time drew near for my operation I began to panic. I had pains in my chest which my GP wondered might even be angina, but they proved to be stress. I was given a date for the operation, and 10 days prior to this I had to go in for tests. Arrangements were made at work for me to have cover and I was to go in on the Wednesday. On the Monday afternoon I had a phone call. My operation had been delayed – my new hip had not arrived.

I was relieved and devastated all in one go. But I saw in this the hand of God. I was not ready for the operation and He needed time to prepare me. From then on I trusted Him and when about a month later I was sent for again, I felt no panic, just an assurance of His will being done. I had a tape of the "Faithful One" chorus which I played to myself as I waited to go to theatre and was perfectly calm. My hip replacement was fine. I was allowed home after 9 days, walking on crutches at first, and after three months I was allowed back to work. I could not believe that I had no pain. After a few months I went in again and had the right hip joint replaced. It was awkward at first as bending is difficult, but I soon learnt different ways of doing things and the pain relief was amazing.

Dad came to see me lots of times and was really helpful and kind to us all. The children kept asking him to meals as we all loved his company so much. It was so good that he was feeling so much better. Dad really enjoyed working in our garden and I found a way in which I could lean over a stool to do weeding, so we spent many hours outside, pottering. I discovered a real interest and love in my garden and Dad taught me a lot.

As I found it easier to walk, I used to walk to my father's house for lunch some days – he lived just around the corner from the school. He made a lovely chicken casserole which I could smell as I approached his house! In the Autumn of 1994 he met a lady of whom he became very fond. We were so pleased for him. He was often very lonely – especially as since his last accident he had not driven. I knew that Mum would have been delighted for him. He kept dropping hints about getting married again; he and Dorothy decided to go on holiday to Majorca early in February. He had only flown once before when he went to Ireland and he had enjoyed the experience. Life was really opening up for him and he had plans to go on a cruise later in the year.

Off they flew to Majorca on the Monday and then very early on the Thursday morning I had a phone call from Dorothy. Dad had had a stroke and was in hospital. She was obviously shocked but she told me the phone number of the clinic and I said I would find out what I could and phone her back. The news was not good. Dad had had a massive stroke and could not be moved. I told Dorothy that I would fly out and started to make arrangements. I did not know how I would manage. Emma said she would come with me, but she too cannot walk far and she had never flown. The daughter of Avril at school, works in a travel agents and so she started to arrange two flights. I had phoned my Auntie Marjorie to tell her what had happened and Sue phoned me back saying she would go with me to Majorca. I was so relieved, as Emma would be useful to remain at home and hold the fort, making any arrangements that would be necessary this end. It was all arranged, my lovely Head teacher gave me an enormous amount of pesetas and on the Friday we travelled up to Heathrow Airport and caught the plane to Palma. We went straight to the clinic and went in to see Dad. He was asleep, he had drips and tubes and his breathing was terrible. He was in a room on his own. The clinic was beautiful – more like a luxury hotel, but I was very upset and asked to see a doctor. It took me quite a while to make the Spanish nurse understand that I wanted to see a doctor and then when she came she only spoke Spanish. I was getting more and more distressed and she sent for someone to translate. A man arrived and said to me "You want I should translate?" "Yes please" I said. He bent down and looked straight at me as the doctor started to talk and it seemed to me that his translation was complete rubbish. For a minute I went quite calm and thought "This is it. I have flipped. This is what it is like when you go mad – the world makes no sense." Then he said "So sorry – I am talking German" I was relieved that I had not completely lost my sanity - but the translation was not good news. The doctor doubted that Dad would ever recognise me again, he had pneumonia and was not expected to live. The stroke had taken place 48 hours before and there had been no improvement.

Sue and I went to the hotel where Dad and Dorothy had been staying and met up with Dorothy. The hotel were so kind and let us stay for nothing until the Monday when Dad's holiday would have ended, and thereafter at considerably reduced rates. Dorothy was very upset and we tried to prepare her for the worst. The next day we went to the clinic and when I walked into his room Dad looked up and said "What are you doing here my lovey?" We were overjoyed: that was certainly more than we had been led to expect. A lot of the time Dad was not lucid – he did not understand he was in Majorca, he did not know what had happened to him and he did not like the nursing staff. At times I was glad that they did not speak very good English so they did not understand what he was saying.

Dorothy went home on the Monday but Sue and I stayed on hoping to go home on the Wednesday. We visited Dad each day – going in for an hour or so, then having a walk around the town, visiting again, sitting by the hospital pool, visiting again, and so on during the day. Dad slept a lot, but we tried to stimulate his brain by asking him what he had planted in my garden and what he put in his chicken casserole. On the Tuesday we were asked not to go home as his pneumonia was very bad and so we cancelled our flight. Yet after that he seemed slightly better – however no movement came back to his right side and he choked when he tried to swallow. At last arrangements were made to fly him back to England on the following Monday. He was to be flown back to Heathrow and then an ambulance would take him to our local hospital, Frenchay. However, we could not fly back to Heathrow with him. Thompsons the tour operator had said that they would give us a free flight if we did not mind where we flew to. They would try to get us to the south of England rather than the north, but they did not fly into Heathrow.

Eventually we flew back to Stanstead Airport and it was really quite easy to catch a shuttle bus to Heathrow and collect the car. We arrived home and after a brief reunion with the family I drove down to see Dad in hospital. I was pleasantly surprised as I had expected the journey to tire him tremendously, but he was not too bad at all. I had grown used to seeing him as he was, but for Emma and Nathan it was a dreadful shock and they were very upset.

Dad had to be isolated for a while as there is an infection rife in foreign hospitals which can cause trouble, not to the carrier, but to any other patients with an open wound. After a few days the test came back negative and so he was able to go into the medical word where they were used to stroke cases. However, Dad did not improve. Whilst he was abroad I had asked God to let him go back to Frenchay as they had a Stroke Unit, and I would be satisfied with what they said. They were disappointed that he had made no real progress and warned me that it was unlikely that he would. At first he thought that he had had a stomach bug and that was why he was so weak and he would not admit that he had had a stroke. He completely ignored the right side of his body – apparently this is common. At one point he even tried to put one slipper on top of another on his left foot, rather than look for the right foot. The human mind is a very complex machine.

Dad used to ask to come home all the time and it got quite upsetting. He would tell people "Sue won't have me home. She must have her reasons, but I wish I could go home." He could not even sit in a chair but he thought he could walk home. Eventually the doctors said to me that we would have to start to look for some sort of full time care for him, but I asked them to tell him and make him understand what was wrong with him, as he had no concept of his limitations. They agreed to have a team meeting about this and come back to me before they spoke to him. That very day Dad said to me "I can't walk Sue, it is no life if you can't walk." The next day he said that while it was alright in hospital, it was no life not being in his own home. No one had to speak to him – he had worked out for himself that he had no quality of life and from then on he quietly slipped away.

I was very proud of my children. They spent as much time with their grandfather as they could. His body had twisted where it had wasted and they rubbed his back and his neck to ease the pain for him. Nathan and Dad had always been very close and teased each other about their girl friends. On the Sunday afternoon Nathan had a girl friend round and Emma and I went in to see Dad. Dad seemed very sleepy and I did not know if he could hear me or not, but I rabbited on in case he could. Running out of things to say, I said "Nathan will be in later – at present he is at home with Stacey. You had better ask him what he has been up to when you see him." Dad made no sign that he had heard me. In the evening I went back in with Nathan. After a while a nurse leaned over Dad to make him more comfortable and he whispered something to her. She turned to Nathan and said "Your grandad wants to know what you have been up to this afternoon with your girlfriend" We did laugh. Dad's face had stopped being able to show emotion, but his spirit was laughing!

When we saw him on the Monday after work he was worse – we all went in and said our good-byes and he died at 2.00 a.m. The hospital phoned me about 10 minutes later, but I had been lying awake since 2.00 a.m. waiting for them to ring. Emma heard the phone and came downstairs and I turned to put the kettle on. God gave me such a vivid picture of my mum and my sister, turning and looking to one side with such loving, happy, welcoming smiles on their faces. I knew who they were welcoming! That picture has kept me going.

Chapter Seventeen

After the funeral came the horrible task of sorting out everything and selling the home. I started in a very half hearted way. Several people offered to help, but I could not get enthusiastic about doing any of it – after Denise had died Mum had kept letters, cards, personal items, etc., after Mum had died Dad had kept the same sort of thing and it brought back their deaths as well as Dad's. On the Sunday morning, the day prior to Dad's funeral, I was sitting in church next to Rosalyn as I usually did. When she was about 12 Ros had baby sat for us, now she was married with two children of her own. For some time they had been renting a bungalow whilst renovating an old house. I asked her how things were going and she said they were about to move into her brother-in-law's small house, sending him back with his parents, as they had been forced to move out of the bungalow as it was needed by the family who owned it. Their own house still had some work to be done on it. She was not happy about this prospect and was worried about her furniture which would have to be stored in a garage.

During the service a thought hit me and I hissed at Ros -"How would you like to live in Dad's house?" "Do you mean it?" she hissed back. During that afternoon Ros and Andrew met me at Dad's house and it was agreed that they would move in. I passed on Dad's suite and a bed to friends who wanted it, freeing space for Ros to bring in some of her furniture. This really was a solution made in Heaven. Ros packed up Dad's things for me – and delivered them to my house where I was able to sort them and decide where to put them. I was so grateful for the help and the spur to get on with it, Ros and Andrew were grateful for the accommodation. We kept arguing about who was helping who the most! Their house was ready just in time for the purchasers of Dad's house to move in on the day they wanted.

One thing we did inherit was Shelley – the tortoise. At first he just hissed at me and we knew he was waiting to go back to Dad's house. He took quite a while to settle and I phoned the vet about him at one stage as I was worried because he would not eat. We even washed his mouth with whisky as one piece of tortoise literature recommended!

However, eventually he started to eat, and eat and we could hardly keep pace with him. I think he quite likes us now and every time I go into the garden he pokes out his head as if he is listening to me when I talk to him. I am very fond of him. He is still an escape artist and Vic and Alan have welded a metal cage for him which we call Colditz – but he still tunnels out occasionally.

Chapter Eighteen

Sometimes I think my life seems like a catalogue of tragedies – but really it is a catalogue of God's goodness and power. I do not know how people manage without a certain knowledge of God's love for them. All the things which have happened in my life have drawn me closer to God. At times my faith may be weak. Recently I felt very weak spiritually and told my minister's wife – she said "Don't worry–I've got faith enough for both of us for now". God accepts that. He does not expect miracles from us – He is the miracle worker. At times depression, tiredness, illness, all can contribute to putting a wall between us and God–but Paul tells us that when we cannot pray the Spirit intercedes for us and we are never separate from God's love. I am very good at remembering little stories but never at remembering where they come from, so I apologise for repeating this story without acknowledging the author. A minister from the south of the USA was visiting a minister from one of the Northern states and as they went out a local lake was covered in ice. "Come on" said the minister from the north "let's go on the ice". The southern minister was too scared – he was not used to frozen lakes where he lived and did not trust the ice. At last he was persuaded to just walk on the edge – just so he could go back and tell his congregation he too had walked on water! He was very glad to get back on the shore. He noticed that one man was sitting right in the centre of the lake and had made a hole and was fishing. Later that day he noticed the same man still sitting there! That made him think. Who had been the safest? The one who had had the greatest faith in the ice? No – they had both been equally safe. So it was not the amount of faith that mattered, rather what the faith was in.

In our Christian lives it is the same – it is not the amount of faith that matters – it is who our faith is in that counts. However, the southern minister also thought the fisherman with the greatest faith had obviously had a lovely day out and enjoyed every minute, whereas he himself had been scared and not enjoyed himself. So while God honours our faith, however small it is, we will enjoy life more when we have total faith and trust in Him. I am looking forward to great things in Heaven. Obviously I want to see those who have gone ahead of me from my own family, and won't it be good to talk to Peter, James and John, and doubting Thomas, always a favourite of mine and what about Martin Luther, William Tyndale and other great men of the past. We won't be in awe of them either. I am looking forward to having no pain, to having freedom of movement. I was talking to Gaynor, our minister's wife one day when she confided that she was tone deaf, so she was looking forward to being able to sing in the heavenly choir in perfect key. I remarked that I had always wanted to be a Tiller Girl or even a Bluebell Girl, able to dance and kick my legs in the air.

Gaynor did not think that there would be a lot of that in Heaven, but I am still hopeful!! I heard a speaker the other day who told us to look around us and let God speak to us. She told us to go away for 15 minutes and see if God spoke to us. I sat where I was and idly looked around. The sound engineer was coiling up wire and laying down more cable. I looked at that and I thought to myself that my life often seems like a bungee jump – God is at the top, but I often seem to be jerking about in all directions. I felt quite strongly that God was saying to me that my life was not like a bungee jump, but that He was in complete control and it was more like abseiling. I might feel like I was jerking about senselessly, but in reality I was just gently pushing against the rock face to steady my descent. I genuinely feel sorry for those who do not feel they need God in their lives. We have been very hard up financially – and God provided. We have needed His help with physical things – God has often undone a handbrake for me when it has been pulled too tight, or turned off a tap when it was difficult. He has sent people to help me when I needed them. He has reassured me of his presence at the very bleakest times of my life, and turned darkness into light. Praise the Lord!

Chapter Nineteen

In June 1996 I started to get pains in my elbows and I was extremely tired – but I thought after the summer holidays I would feel much better and ready for another school year. We had a lovely holiday in Cornwall, but the pain in my arms got worse and my right arm kept locking. We went to stay in a farmhouse on Bodmin Moor with our friends, Alan and Shirley and their big black labrador, Duke. Daisy was in her element and kept forcing her old bones to keep up with Duke, usually towing me along on the end of her lead – no wonder my arms complained!

September came and the new school year. After about one week I knew I could not go on. I was so tired at the end of each day, my arms ached and locked periodically. Instead of enjoying my job I was dreading being given any typing to do and in October I went to see my GP, who advised seeking early retirement on health grounds.

When I told Emma and Nathan I was finishing work they immediately asked if we would be moving to Cornwall. We had always said that we would retire there, but this was quite a bit sooner than we had planned. As they were both working I was surprised that they seemed so keen on the idea and after much talk and much prayer we decided to put our house on the market with a view to eventually moving to Cornwall. As the house was an ex-council house, the kitchen had been adapted and so would need to be completely replaced before anyone else could use it, and the situation was not on a bus route so any purchaser would have to have their own transport, we realised that we would have difficulty in selling it. However, we approached estate agents in Cornwall and asked them to send us information about bungalows with small gardens. Emma and I planned to go and stay with my cousin for a few days, and if we had information on any properties we liked, we would take a look at them. A few days before our proposed visit to Cornwall we received details of two properties – one with a stable block which Vic immediately fell in love with, as it would have made a workshop for him, and one I fell in love with which seemed to be a large bungalow with a small garden.

The estate agent put the 'For Sale' notice in our garden a few hours before Emma and I left for Cornwall, and we were surprised by a knock on the door from our neighbour in a rented property to the right of our house, just as we were on the point of leaving. Vic was able to phone us later to say that the neighbours intended to make an offer the next day! This they did, so Emma and I could look at properties with real intent. The bungalow Vic was interested in proved to have been taken off the market and was on a steep slope anyway. The bungalow I liked was perfect and after phoning Vic and contacting a builder friend, who checked that he could alter the kitchen for us, we made an offer which was accepted. My cousin's husband made a video of the bunga-low so that Vic could see what we were buying. Vic trusted my judgement and I am happy to say that he loves it as much as I do.

The person selling the house was so helpful and the whole move went like clockwork—confirmation that God's hand was on the situation. What has truly amazed me, although I should not be surprised, is confirmation that God had this all planned for us years ago. Emma met the son of the couple who had the bungalow built and he told her that they had had it designed specifically with a wheelchair in mind in case either of them or their parents were ever in a situation where they needed to use one. They didn't and left the bungalow, nor did the next couple who lived there, but Vic does and God had prepared for that!

As we settle into our new life here in Cornwall I often think about my father and wonder what he would have made of us returning to his home land. His remaining brother and sister think he would be glad. I think perhaps he would—I'm sure he would have liked the bungalow, so much easier to manage than the house, and the garden, pleasant for sitting out without being a chore to maintain.

I felt no qualms at leaving our house. I had always loved it but it seemed time to move on, and I did not feel the need to say good bye to it. I suppose all that was precious was going with me—my family, Daisy, and the few possessions which hold memories. It was different when Dad's house was sold.

The night before Dad's house was to pass to its new owner I went around to say goodbye. Although I had only actually lived there for 6 years, it was the family home to me. It was here that I could visualise best all those I have lost.

As I drew up outside I nearly turned around and went home again, but it was something I had to do, and I forced myself to go inside.

I went upstairs first, to the bedroom which had been mine. The smallest room, where mum used to bring me breakfast in bed as she hated me to go to work without anything inside me. What a lazy toad I was!

The front bedroom which used to be mum's and dad's. I can remember taking them a cup of tea in bed. It was a real struggle for me to get up the stairs carrying a cup, but I did do it occasionally. The wallpaper dad had hung just before mum was ill was still on the wall. He took ages to get three drops up and then called us for our opinion. Mum and I looked at each other, both thinking the same thing. Which of us was going to tell him he had put it on upside down! He was not pleased!!

The back bedroom had been Denise's—I could not remember where she had had her bed, which wall it had been against, or even what colour it had been. Dad had slept sometimes in the back and sometimes in the front, and I could only visualise the room as he had used it.

The bathroom had a new suite since I left home so it did not seem so familiar to me. The front room downstairs brought back lots of happy memories. Christmases where Dad, Vic, Terry, Denise and I would gather round the organ whilst mum played carols and we all sang. Or mum would play while we played 'pass the parcel'. The room was empty, but I could still see the furniture and all those so dear to me sitting there. It was in this room that Vic asked Dad's permission to marry me. I could see my cousin Terry sitting in the chair with Emma on his lap when she was a tiny baby.

Next I went into the kitchen where so clearly I could see mum standing at the stove, getting out the jam tarts on Sundays. I could see dad dishing up one of his chicken casseroles. I could see one of Denise's old boyfriends who had come to see her on his motor bike and left his helmet on the draining board. When she told him she had finished with him, he was so upset he picked up the mixing bowl and almost put it on his head by mistake!

I can see Auntie Marjorie saying "Well, I'll be off" and walking off into the pantry instead of out of the back door!

I can remember that awful day when Denise and Terry were in the kitchen and Terry was talking and put his hand down on the cooker, when the ring had only just been turned off. He had thick burns in the shape of the cooker ring for weeks.

There is a toilet and washbasin just outside the kitchen door, and I can see cousin Terry fixing up a combined light and heater there for mum when she was dying, not knowing that he was dying himself.

I went out into the garden and took some more cuttings of the Daphne which mum had been given when she left the hospital, hoping that this time they would take. I looked in the greenhouse where Dad happily spent so much of his time but everything was dead and neglected. The apple tree was full of apples. The pear tree had more fruit than usual, the pear tree which we bought for dad's birthday one year. We left it outside our house and when we were out he called over. He went back to mum and said that he had found a pear tree at our house and (being pretty sure where we would plant it) had almost started to dig the hole ... So it was the pear tree that he almost never had.

I had been putting off going into the dining room. The room which was used the most, and the room where my mum died. I expected to feel overwhelmed but I didn't. There was a sense of peace in that room. There were no ghosts, just happy memories, even of her last days. Perhaps in many ways they were the ultimate in days – days when I was increasingly privileged to share with her a glimpse of heaven, until that day when she actually stepped over its threshold leaving me behind.

Chapter Twenty

Emma and Nathan have now grown up into their late teens and with the years have come all the sorts of problems that teenagers have, plus the ones brought about by our decision to have children and pass on the gene which causes restricted growth, and these are the problems which at times threaten to overwhelm me, as it makes me question the validity of our choice. I have to keep reminding myself that this was a choice made by God and that they are on loan to us to nurture for His purposes.

They both have to cope with being different from their peers, and to a large extent they have coped well. Emma has now studied to become a personal assistant – following in her mother's footsteps! At one time she wanted to go to university to study Theology but either she gave up on her A-levels or they gave up on her, either way the results indicated that she was not destined for an academic career! However, although she was happy on the course she was doing and did have a job with a local newspaper in Bristol, she has been unable to find similar work in Cornwall and may work in a local factory. She remains committed to her Lord. She went to Albania in the summer of 1995 to evangelise and work among the children, and enjoyed it tremendously. She was struck by the way she had to rely on God for protection every minute of the day and found it difficult to settle when she came back into the self-reliant world we have created for ourselves in the western world. She waits for God to show her where she should go in life. She has a lovely singing voice, is good at drama and loves to lead Bible studies, encouraging young people to really delve into the truths which are there for everyone who looks.

Nathan left school at 16 with 6 O-level passes at GCSE and went on a course leading to a computer qualification. He had a job for a while as a trainee engineer but that did not work out as he found it too demanding physically, so he is now looking for something to do. Jobs for 17-year-olds are few and far between in Cornwall, especially with Nathan's height restriction. So it looks as if he will be back studying for more qualifications. He has a wide circle of friends, a lovely girlfriend, and seems to have come through the "teenage grumps". He is a wonderful help especially to his father. As I went to work when Nathan was young, he has a special relationship with his father and this is very precious to both of them.

For several years when both were fragile teenagers, we had to walk on eggshells, but that time is now over; it is so wonderful to hold conversations with a reasonable expectation that noone will say something which someone else takes objection to! I don't know whether our teenagers have been worse than others—they obviously have had more pressures that most—but we have come out of the other side safely and for that I thank God.

I hope that Emma and Nathan find fulfilment in all aspects of their lives. Whether or not they find a life partner, what their careers will be, where they will live, remains to be seen, but more importantly my desire is that they continue with the Lord, for what is there without Him?

Vic still has days when he is in a lot of pain, days when his legs go into spasm and almost throw him from his chair, however his faith remains as always. His faith is very simple and uncomplicated—he leaves the theological debate to Emma and me! In spite of his problems he always did the weekly shopping, most of the cooking and most of the ironing, whilst I was working, and we now do it together. We are enjoying our retirement!

So what of the future? My life goes on, and I am trying to keep my eyes on the Glory that lies ahead . Paul says in 2 Cor. 4 that while our bodies are decaying, inwardly we are being renewed. I don't know about you, but I hate looking in the mirror and seeing yet more lines on my face, being told I need a stronger prescription for my glasses or finding new grey hairs! But these things do not matter as they are so temporary compared with what is to come.

It is a constant source of wonder to me that the Bible has so much in it! After 48 years, one would think that I had read most of it and it would be boring, but there is something new every time I open it. My grandmother and my mother had Sunday School prize books, which I now have. These books written seventy or eighty years ago are so dated that, although they have a spiritual theme, they have become amusing in their antiquated way of writing and the sentiments they indulge. Why then does the Bible seem so relevant today? After all it was written long before the Sunday School prize books. The only conclusion I can come to is that it is the word of God. There is direct information from God written there for every situation in which you can find yourself. Vic recently bought me a Life Application Bible—they are expensive, but such a help to understanding the more difficult passages. The more you read your Bible, the more it becomes a friend, familiar pages open themselves to you and you know exactly where to turn when you need help. Bible study notes are good, but a Bible study with other Christians is excellent.

My purpose in writing my story is to show you that I have a wonderful Lord and Master who loves me, looks after me and protects me and will continue to do so until the day I join Him in glory. He can and will do the same for you if you let Him. You may never have to face some of the things which have happened in my life, and in a way you will be the poorer for this. It is because I knew from an early age that I could not manage on my own that I have trusted Him to see me through my life and all it has brought. Sometimes it seems that we only look for God when we cannot fall any further down. I have had times of great depression and even doubt, but He sees me through even these. If I were physically and mentally stronger perhaps I might have been tempted to try to live without Him. I would have failed just as miserably, but I might have tried! So I thank God for my weakness: "Blessed are the poor in spirit for theirs is the kingdom of Heaven."

Jesus told a parable of the workers in the vineyard. The owner of the vineyard went to the market place and took some men on at dawn to do a day's work for him, promising them a denarius in payment. The owner went back to the market place at lunch time and again took on more men promising them the same amount, and the same thing happened at tea time. Each time the men were promised the same amount. I have often heard preachers say that this shows that God's idea of fairness may not be what we perceive to be just. I always look at it another way – I'm like that! I think those men would have been worried about how to feed their families. Those that were taken on first worked well because they were relieved that they would be able to provide. Those that were taken on at lunch time had all the morning to worry about how they would survive and those who were not taken on until later had even longer to worry. They would have been so relieved that they could provide at the end of the day that they would have worked really hard. But they had most of the day to worry and cope alone.

Our lives are like that – we try on our own and make a real mess – those of us who come to the Lord early in life know that we can put all our cares on Him and He will provide. Like the men in the vineyard, we might stop for a while, but then we get back to working for Him. Some might struggle on until the very end of their lives before they turn to Him, but He is just as faithful and has the same reward for them. The Kingdom of Heaven is for all those who God calls. Don't delay – ask God into your life today.